Genio:

The Story of Italian Genius

Morris Berman

Also by Morris Berman

Social Change and Scientific Organization

Trilogy on human consciousness:
   The Reenchantment of the World
   Coming to Our Senses
   Wandering God: A Study in Nomadic Spirituality

Trilogy on the American empire:
   The Twilight of American Culture
   Dark Ages America: The Final Phase of Empire
   Why America Failed: The Roots of Imperial Decline

A Question of Values (essays)
Destiny (fiction)
Counting Blessings (poetry)
Spinning Straw Into Gold (memoir)
The Man Without Qualities (fiction)
Are We There Yet? (essays)

Neurotic Beauty: An Outsider Looks at Japan

Genio:

The Story of Italian Genius

Morris Berman

ECHO POINT BOOKS & MEDIA, LLC
Brattleboro, Vermont

Published by Echo Point Books & Media
Brattleboro, Vermont
www.EchoPointBooks.com

All rights reserved.
Neither this work nor any portions thereof may be reproduced, stored in a retrieval system, or transmitted in any capacity without written permission from the publisher.

Copyright © 2019, 2021 by Morris Berman

Genio: The Story of Italian Genius / 1st edition
ISBN: 978-1-62654-883-1 (casebound)
       978-1-64837-039-7 (paperback)

Interior design by Jeffrey P. Fisher

Cover design by John Trotter

Cover image: *Apollo and Daphne by* Bernini,
           at Galleria Borghese, Rome, Italy

The men who produce works of genius are not those who live in the most delicate atmosphere, whose conversation is the most brilliant or their culture the most extensive, but those who have had the power, ceasing suddenly to live only for themselves, to transform their personality into a sort of mirror, in such a way that their life…is reflected by it, genius consisting in reflecting power and not in the intrinsic quality of the scene reflected.
—Proust, *Within a Budding Grove*

Perhaps it was in this, I said to Albertine, this unknown quality of a unique world which no other [artist or writer] had ever yet revealed, that the most authentic proof of genius lies, even more than in the content of the work itself.
—Proust, *The Captive*

Contents

List of Illustrations vii
Acknowledgments and Credits viii
Preface: The Creation of "Space"................................ xi
1. Bernini: Miracle in Marble 1
2. Caravaggio: Drama in Oil 11
3. Fellini: Magic and Pasta 21
4. St. Francis: A Fool for God 37
5. Machiavelli: Politics as Science 49
6. Gramsci: Mind over Matter 59
7. Marinetti: Future Perfect 73
Epilogue: My Italy 89
Notes 91
About the Author 105

List of Illustrations

1. Gianlorenzo Bernini, self-portrait
2. *The Goat Amalthea with the Infant Jupiter and a Faun*
3. The *David*
4. *Apollo and Daphne*
5. *The Ecstasy of St. Teresa*
6. Portrait of Caravaggio by Ottavio Leoni
7. *Boy Bitten by a Lizard*
8. *The Cardsharps*
9. *The Calling of St. Matthew*
10. *David with the Head of Goliath*
11. Federico Fellini
12. Giulietta Masina as Gelsomina in *La strada*
13. Marcello Mastroianni and Anita Ekberg in *La dolce vita*
14. Surreal sequence of Marcello Mastroianni in *8½*
15. Caravaggio, *Saint Francis in Prayer*
16. Portrait of Machiavelli by Santi di Tito
17. Antonio Gramsci
18. Filippo Tommaso Marinetti
19. Antonio Sant'Elia, *La Città nuova*
20. Giacomo Balla, *Dynamism of a Dog in Motion*
21. Ivo Pannaggi, *Speeding Train*

Acknowledgments and Credits

I wish to thank John Trotter for the time and effort he devoted to the selection and preparation of the illustrations, and to Jeffrey Fisher for similar dedication regarding layout and design. Rebeca Martínez also helped with the photos, and Beatrice Scaccia was generous with her support and enthusiasm. Grazie mille, amici; every author needs these kinds of friends.

Credits for the illustrations are as follows:
- Plates 1, 6-11, 13, 15-17, and 19-20 are in the public domain. Numbers 6 and 9 require the following annotation: https://commons.wikimedia.org/wiki/Commons:Copyright_tags#United_States
- Source for Plate 2: https://en.wikipedia.org/wiki/The_Goat_Amalthea_with_the_Infant_Jupiter_and_a_Faun Photographer: Peter80
- Source for Plate 3: Beth Harris and Steven Zucker, "Gian Lorenzo Bernini, *David*," in *Smarthistory*, 12 July 2015, https://smarthistory.org/bernini-david-2/
- Source for Plates 4 (and cover illustration) and 5: https://en.wikipedia.org/wiki/Gian_Lorenzo_Bernini Photographer: Joaquim Alves Gaspar. Changes made to Plate 5: The image was cropped.
- Source for Plate 12: article by Juan Carlos González at https://www.tiempodecine.co/web/gelsomina-nos-mira-la-strada-de-federico-fellini/
- Source for Plate 14: article by Lorna May at http://www.itchysilk.com/intothecuttingroom-with-federico-fellini-and-8%C2%BD-1963/

- Source for Plate 18: http://www.libros-books-amazonia.com/2015/12/biografia-de-filippo-tommaso-marinetti.html
- Source for Plate 21: http://www.artandantiquesmag.com/2014/02/italian-futurists/201403_italian_02/

Every effort was made to locate the sources for permissions for items not in the public domain. We ask any publisher in possession of such information to contact us, and we shall be happy to include the appropriate credit in future editions of the book.

Preface: The Creation of "Space"

The idea for *Genio: The Story of Italian Genius* was born in a moment of epiphany in September of 2017, when I came across Bernini's sculpture, *Apollo and Daphne*, in the Galleria Borghese in Rome. It's possible I had seen it during my previous visit to Rome, in 1969; I can't remember. But what a young man sees in a work of art is likely to be very different from what an older man sees. In any case, as an older man I was transfixed: the beautiful tresses of Daphne shown in marble, in the act of being transformed into laurel leaves. The dynamic quality of this event, the capturing of movement and metamorphosis in marble, was clearly the work of a genius; and somewhat later, sitting in a café on Piazza Navona with a friend of mine, I reflected out loud on whether movement and transformation—the creation of space, understood metaphorically—might be the source of Italy's great cultural contribution to the world. Were these elements present in the films of Fellini? In the spirituality of St. Francis? In the political analysis of Machiavelli, or Antonio Gramsci? I was intrigued by this possibility.(1)

Writing about the Enlightenment philosopher and historian Giambattista Vico, Isaiah Berlin commented that "Vico saw in Homer not an individual who wrote the *Iliad* and the *Odyssey*, but the national genius of the Greek people itself, as it articulates its vision of its own experience over the centuries."(2) What might the national genius of the Italian people be? Well, more than one thing, I'm sure; but I'm convinced that the ability—

whether in art, religion, or political theory—to transform and expand a static situation, thereby generating a wider degree of freedom, is high up on the list of factors. Of course, this could also apply to German music, or French literature, for all I know; but my interest in this little book is how it plays out to make Italian culture the envy of the Western world. I do not, however, intend to be exhaustive, or especially scholarly. *Genio* is a collection of cameos, so to speak, ones that demonstrate the power of a single motif to explain how aliveness, and beauty in its widest sense, come to be.

So if Daphne gets transformed into a tree, Gramsci liberates Marxism from its dogmatic categories into an analytical tool that credits the superstructure (culture, the world of the mind) with as much political significance or revolutionary potential as the base (economy, the mode of production). St. Francis, in his turn, revitalizes a Catholic Church that had betrayed its origins, steeped as it was in corruption and hierarchical rigidity. Fellini breaks with Italian neorealism and, with the help of Jungian psychology, turns film into a kind of dream medium, practically precipitating a revolution in Western consciousness. And so on.

How to define genius? In general, I would argue that a genius is someone whose work permanently alters the perceptual landscape. But Italian genius, I believe, does this in a particular way, and this is what I wish to explore in this book.

M.B.
Mexico City, 2018

One

Bernini: Miracle in Marble

> In earth she stood, white thighs embraced by climbing
> Bark, her white arms branches, her fair head swaying
> In a cloud of leaves; all that was Daphne bowed
> In the stirring of the wind, the glittering green
> Leaf twined within her hair and she was laurel.
> —Ovid, *Metamorphoses*, Book I

Gianlorenzo Bernini's work is so stunning, so astonishing, that in the face of it we are left with one overriding question: Where did such an individual come from? Given Bernini's transformative impact on European sculpture, it becomes hard to resist the "heroic" version of history, according to which single, remarkable individuals alter the course of human events by the sheer force of their talent or personality. On this version, history becomes something of an accident: absent the birth of Galileo, for example, the Scientific Revolution of the seventeenth century would never have occurred. These people emerge *ex nihilo*, like Athena from the head of Zeus. The German philosopher Hegel called such persons "world historical individuals," but this phenomenon was, for him, hardly accidental. Rather, these people were akin to lightning rods, attracting and condensing the major tendencies of their age, and altering that age through their "resonance" with it. This is not to diminish Galileo's genius in any way—it was quite real—but rather to argue that both the internal development of physics and astronomy, and the social and religious events swirling around Italy ca. 1600, had in effect made someone like Galileo not just possible, but probably inevitable. The same can be said of Bernini, around the same time and within the same country.

The crux of Bernini's genius—the translation of movement into hard rock so as to join the spiritual and the sensual into a single dynamic expression—lay at the heart of the Baroque "revolution" of the early seventeenth century. Franco Mormando, Bernini's most recent English-language biographer, writes that by this time, the cautious style of ecclesiastical art, which is to say the art of the Counter-Reformation of the previous fifty years, was over. The new Baroque style emphasized movement, light, and emotion. The Swiss art historian, Heinrich Wölfflin, identified it as "movement imported into mass." The Baroque departed from the previous "Mannerist" fashion, which put its emphasis on the artificial (as opposed to the natural) and the intellectual. In contrast, the Baroque made an appeal to the senses. Thus another art historian, Rudolf Wittkower, asserted that the "transmission of emotive experience was the main object of Baroque religious imagery." In general, it was the goal of the Baroque era to represent movement in its artwork.(1)

Bernini was the apotheosis of all this. His son Domenico, one of his earliest biographers (1713), remarked that his father "did not work the marble but devoured it." And when he worked, said Domenico, "he seemed to be in a state of ecstasy and as if he were sending out through his eyes his own spirit in order to give life to his blocks of stone." While he didn't quite approach Mozart in precocity, he came pretty close. *The Goat Amalthea with the Infant Jupiter and a Faun* (Plate 2) was probably done in 1611-12, when Bernini was thirteen or fourteen, although it has also been dated as early as 1609—when he was eleven. As with Mozart's first composition at age five, the mind boggles. The central conceit of most of Bernini's work, namely the capturing of a frozen moment of transformation, is already present here: the faun, or satyr, raises a shell containing milk from the goat, which is about to spill over the edge. This "persistent rendering of a transitory moment" (Wittkower) is what Bernini became famous for; there is a freedom and energy in his work that sets him apart from his contemporaries. The concept that Bernini chose for representation in his art, says Wittkower, is "always the moment of dramatic climax."(2)

This is clearly the case in Bernini's statue of David (Plate 3), which is a far cry from the David given to us by Michelangelo. What we see in Bernini's version is the torque of the body, tense and wound up before slinging the stone. "We are tempted to duck," comments biographer Charles Scribner. A key technique being employed here is the rendering of movement via *contrapposto*, or dynamic juxtaposition. In this "counterpoise," the shoulders move in one direction, and the hips in the other. Scribner continues: "The psychological intensity is heightened by the anticipation of violence; latent power is momentarily suspended," and the surrounding space feels electrically charged—an effect Bernini cultivated throughout his career.(3)

Turning now to my favorite, *Apollo and Daphne* (Plate 4), it would seem that this work is everyone's favorite as well. Thus the contemporary sculptor Peter Rockwell writes, "any sculptor who looks at Bernini's *Apollo and Daphne* can only come away astonished." "Never before," he adds, "had marble statues been so palpably alive." In the *David,* we see the subject (Bernini, in fact) biting his lip; in *Apollo and Daphne,* we see the fear expressed by Daphne's wide open mouth.(4)

The myth of Apollo and Daphne goes back to the third century B.C., possibly earlier. Ovid's version (A.D. 8) can be found in Book I of the *Metamorphoses* (see epigraph to this chapter). In the story, Apollo insults Eros (Cupid), so Eros pierces him with an arrow of gold. As a result, he falls madly in love with Daphne. But in the meantime, Eros pierces her with an arrow of lead, so that she is repulsed by Apollo. Apollo chases her; to escape, she appeals to her father, a river god, to intervene. He obliges, turning her into a laurel tree the very moment that Apollo catches up with her.(5)

Again, movement, dynamism, and the transformative moment, are the keys here. Apollo stands on one leg; drapery flows around him; Daphne's hair is flying away. Ovid says that Daphne fled "swifter than the wind's breath"; Apollo follows her in "divine pursuit." Whereas Renaissance art was interested in stability, what Bernini gives us is change, motion, disorder. The British journalist Hamish Bowles calls the sculpture "frankly miraculous," while art historian Howard Hibbard regards it as a "hallucinatory vision." As for Wittkower, he asserts that works like the *David* and *Apollo and Daphne* "demonstrate an amazing process of emancipation which is hardly equaled in the whole history of sculpture." The figures display "a transitory moment, the climax of an action." Instead of the self-contained pieces of the past, we see figures striding through space.(6)

Finally, we come to what might be Bernini's most famous work, the *Ecstasy of St.Teresa* (Plate 5), which the great perfectionist referred to as "the least bad thing I ever did." Indeed. The sculpture is overwhelming in its frank sexuality—both then and now. We see St. Teresa in a state of rapture; she seems to be floating in midair. It is also, as with the works discussed above, a depiction of the subject at the instant of transformation—"a moment," says Simon Schama, "that wavers between mystery and indecency." The orgasm is physical, but also spiritual: "the visualization of pure bliss," and the portrayal of a saint "in a way no one else had ever dared." "One searches in vain," adds Mormando, "for another artistic recreation of this scene charged with the same degree of sexual electricity."(7)

With Bernini, movement can be found wherever one looks. When he sculpted portrait busts, he asked his subjects (including Louis XIV) to walk around, so that he could catch the individual in motion, rather than just sitting still in a chair. In the famous fountains he designed for Rome, he used powerful streams, so as to create a "continuous movement of the rushing and murmuring water" (Wittkower). And Bernini himself, during his lifetime, was in constant motion, conjuring works of art with amazing speed. Nearly to the time of his death, he lived in a kind of whirlwind. "All of his works," writes one observer, "give the sense of being a snapped moment of stillness in a frenzy of motion." He gave us a new idea of what a work of art could do, and as a result, art has never been the same.(8)

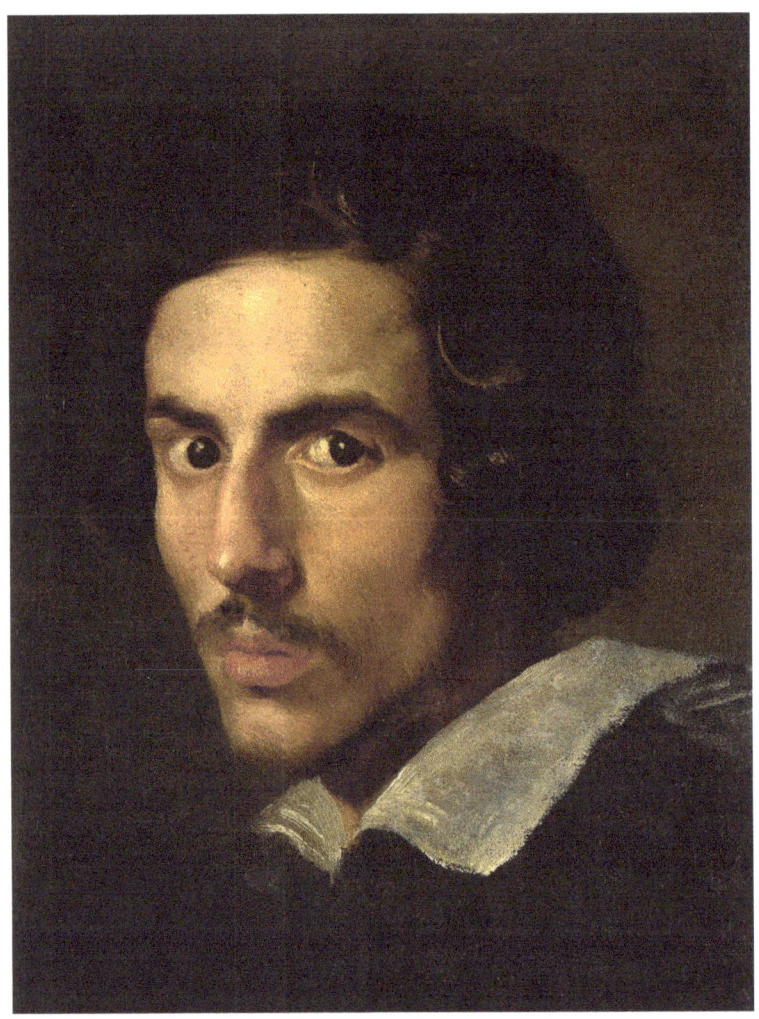

1. Gianlorenzo Bernini, self-portrait

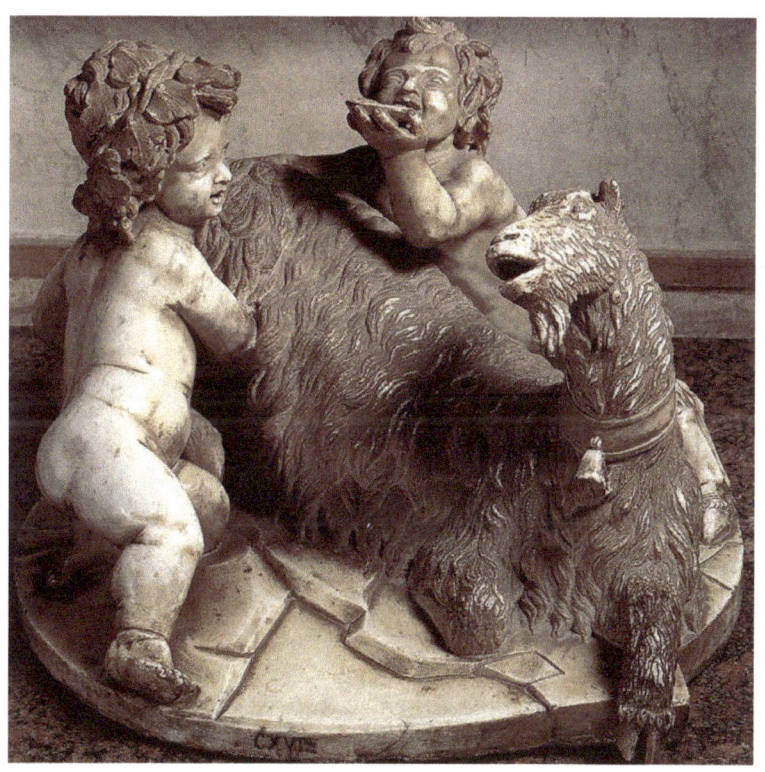

2. The Goat Amalthea with the Infant Jupiter and a Faun

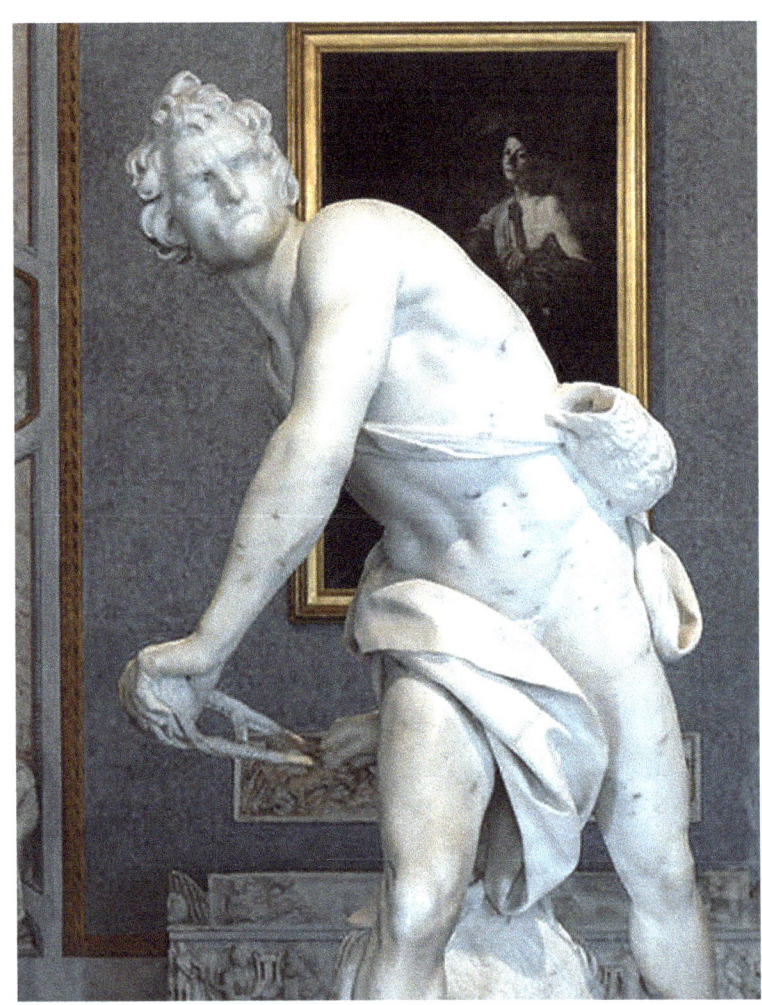

3. The *David*

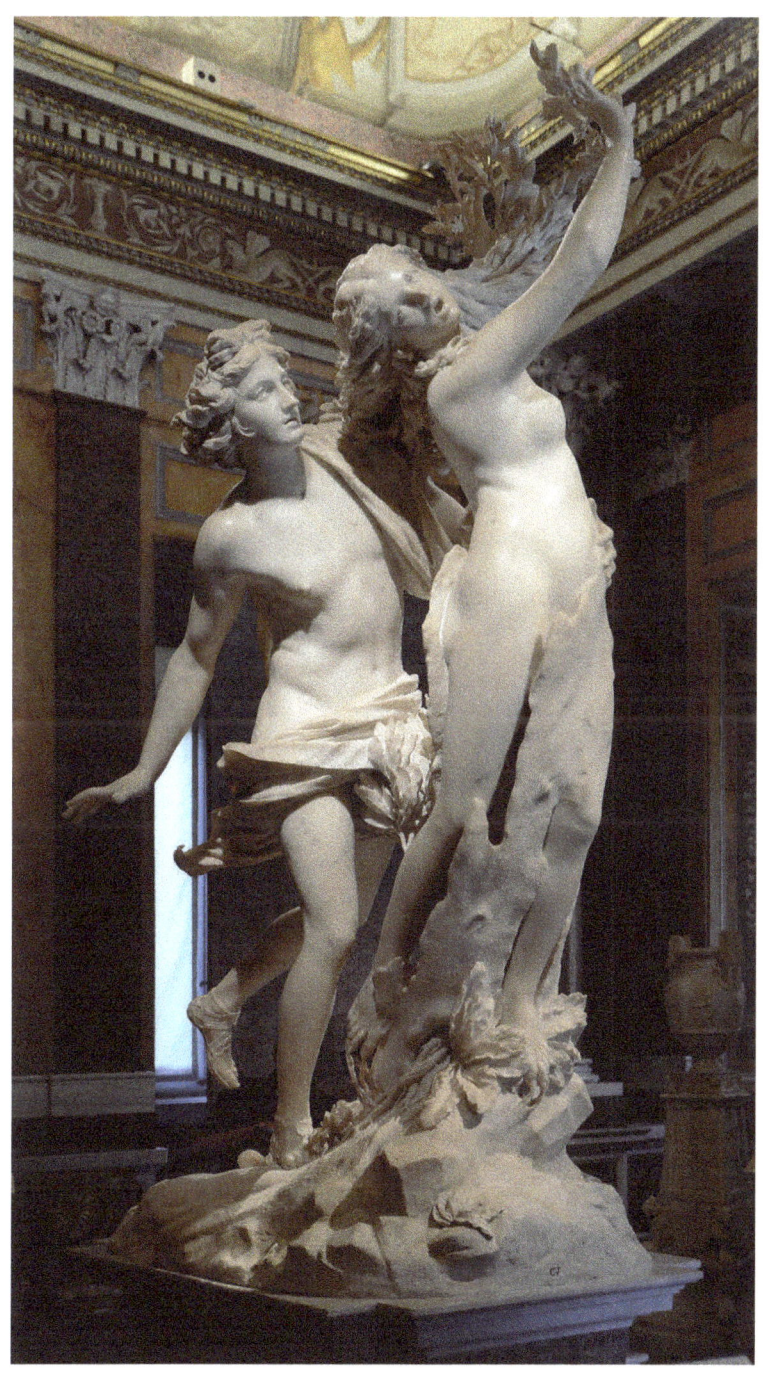

4. Apollo and Daphne

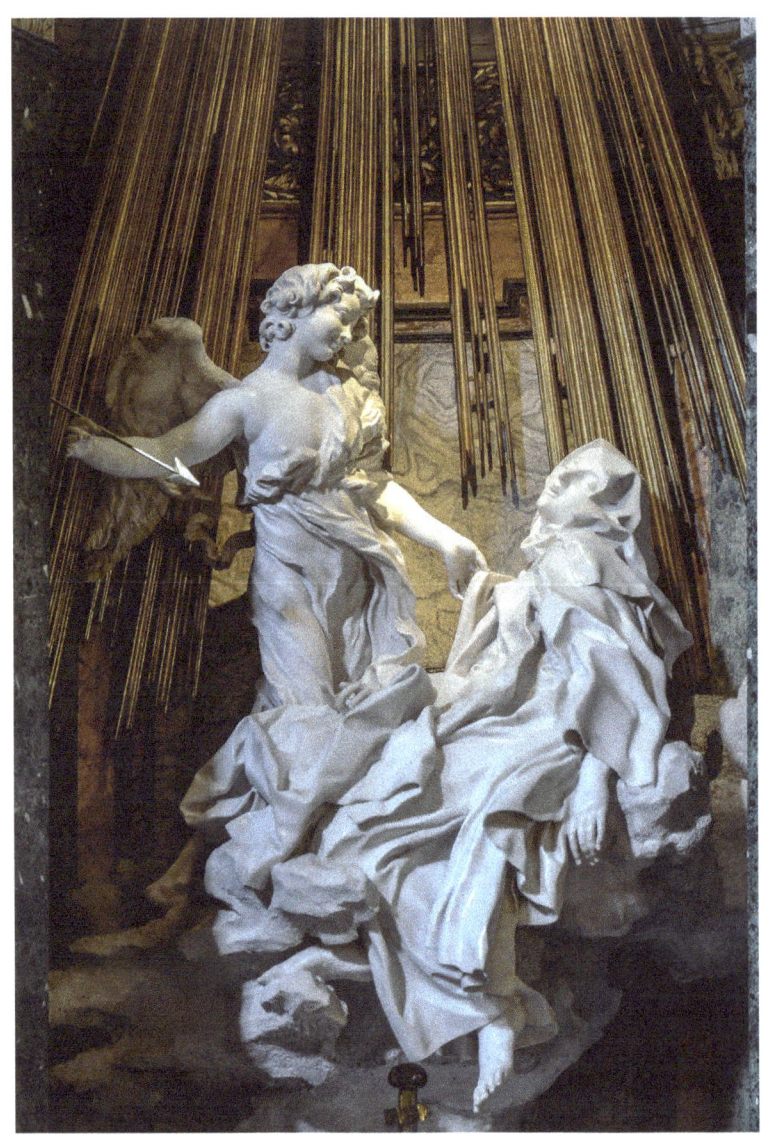

5. *The Ecstasy of St. Teresa*

Two

Caravaggio: Drama in Oil

Initially I related to [his] paintings because of the moment that he chose to illuminate in the story. The Conversion of [St.] Paul, Judith Beheading Holofernes: he was choosing a moment that was not the absolute moment of the beginning of the action, it's during he action...You sort of come upon the scene midway and you're immersed in it....It was like modern staging in a film. It was as if we had just come in the middle of [a] scene and it was all happening.... He would have made a great filmmaker...The Calling of [St.] Matthew, in New York!
—Martin Scorsese, interview, 2005

What begins in the work of Caravaggio is, quite simply, modern painting.
—Art historian André Berne-Joffroy

The same—that he lived in a whirlwind, and that he changed the face of European art—might be said of Caravaggio as well. Like Bernini, Caravaggio sought out the transformative moment, the high point of the drama being depicted. "Looking at his pictures," writes the art critic Andrew Graham-Dixon, "is like looking at the world by flashes of lightning."(1)

Full name: Michelangelo Merisi da Caravaggio, born in Milan in 1571 (some sources say in the town of Caravaggio, near Milan). Actually, saying that his life was characterized by movement is a rather severe understatement. It was not merely turbulent, it was chaotic and violent, even including a homicide and flights from the law. In both art and life, he was always in revolt, and died exhausted, a tormented soul, at age thirty-eight.

Caravaggio left Milan for Rome in 1592, after quarrels that led to the wounding of a police officer. Similar street brawls characterized his life in Rome, and transcripts of his police records go on for several pages. In 1606 he killed a young man in a sword fight. It may have been unintentional, but he was branded an outlaw and fled to Naples. Soon after, he moved on to Malta, was imprisoned in 1608, escaped, and made his way to Sicily, where his behavior became increasingly erratic. In 1609 he was caught in an ambush that disfigured his face, and in 1610 he died in Tuscany, of a fever or possibly lead poisoning. (2)

The drama in Caravaggio's life managed to find expression in his art, in a number of ways. It is not surprising that Bernini spent hundreds of hours studying and copying Caravaggio's work, until he was able to translate the latter's technique of capturing a frozen, dynamic moment in three dimensions. The sensual vitality of Bernini's sculpture, and his use of chiaroscuro —"the emotionally charged and spiritualized contrast of light and shadow"—have much of their origins in Caravaggio's paintings as well.(3)

The *Boy Bitten by a Lizard* (Plate 7), done when Caravaggio was around twenty-four years of age, clearly displays his trademark of "compressed drama" (Graham-Dixon). You can almost hear the boy scream, as he tenses up and pulls back his hand. He was reaching out toward a selection of fruit when suddenly, a lizard sunk its fangs into his middle finger (in reality, lizards have no teeth). Also notable, and characteristic of Caravaggio, is that the boy is no one special, a person without rank or status. Caravaggio was interested in people he found in the rough, in the streets, and he knew the streets quite well.(4)

Another moment of compressed drama is captured in *The Cardsharps* (Plate 8), also painted in the closing years of the sixteenth century. It is, according to Graham-Dixon, one of the most innovative paintings created in Europe at this time. Another biographer, Helen Langdon, writes that the painting "startled the classical art world with a story from the everyday world," and was, in addition, particularly "strong in the sense of a moment seen." It shows a dandy of sorts, a young aristocrat, about to be cheated out of his money by two con men. It plays on the popular fear of "a world turned upside down," in which low-life characters—again, street folk—win, and aristocrats get taken to the cleaners; although there is a hint of some sympathy for these characters as well (who are, like Caravaggio, poor). The painting was an immediate success, and one wealthy art collector, Cardinal Francesco Maria del Monte, was so taken by it (along with a similar one, called *The Gypsy Fortune-Teller*), that he not only bought it, but also invited Caravaggio to live in his palace. Meanwhile, the "trickster" genre took off, to be copied by numerous artists across Europe, including Rembrandt.(5)

Caravaggio's first major religious commission, *The Calling of St. Matthew*, was obtained for him by del Monte, and completed in 1600 (Plate 9). Matthew is a tax collector; he sits in a dingy room somewhere in Rome, surrounded by four other men of the same profession. In the bible (Matthew 9:9), all that happens is that Jesus enters the room and singles Matthew out: "Follow me." Caravaggio, says Graham-Dixon, painted the exact moment of conversion at the heart of this extremely compressed narrative. Matthew is astonished, points to himself as if to say, "Who, me?" Light shines on his face, while Christ, in the shadows, "fixes the tax-collector with a hypnotizingly intense stare." There is no doubt as to the outcome here: Matthew will get up and go; his fate is sealed.(6)

The mood here is similar to that of the tavern in *The Cardsharps*—seedy and mercenary. "Christ brings light into this darkness," comments Graham-Dixon, "just as he brings illumination and divine purpose to Matthew's dreary, money-grubbing existence....It is the light of ordinary mundane reality, yet it is also the light of God." Truth be told, it is like a fragment of a dream, a dream of suddenly being called away from a life of vice, without any context or explanation, and into that divine light. Again, a metamorphosis: Matthew the tax collector becomes a different person, someone else. "In an era passionately concerned with personal salvation, and with the individual's call to God," says Helen Langdon, "the picture, so rooted in contemporary reality, had immense power."(7)

There is one more painting I wish to discuss. Recall the homicide of 1606, briefly referred to above. Caravaggio killed a man in a duel (sword fight); was sentenced in absentia to permanent exile from Rome; and had a bounty placed on his head as a condemned murderer. As a result, he wasted no time fleeing the city, eventually settling in Naples, which was under Spanish rule at the time. During the first few months of his exile, he painted what would become one of his most famous works, *David with the Head of Goliath* (Plate 10).(8)

Again, we have a snapshot of a crucial moment: David has just slain Goliath and holds up the latter's severed head, from which blood is still pouring out of the neck. The head, notes Graham-Dixon, seems to be screaming in death agony. David (modelled by Caravaggio's assistant Francesco Boneri, also known as Cecco) looks sadly upon it "with an almost Christ-like expression." But the real knockout punch here is the head, which is that of Caravaggio himself, *in extremis*. All of the torment of Caravaggio's soul has been concentrated in his face. In the BBC documentary, "Power of Art," Simon Schama tells us that "David and Goliath" is a self-portrait unlike any other painted before. It reveals a desolate vision, one imbued with self-knowledge. In all of us, Caravaggio seems to be saying, there is a David and a Goliath, and they aren't on very good terms. Early Freud (or Jung), one might say.(9)

Caravaggio, like Bernini, is almost too powerful to be believed. Like the latter, he worked at great speed, without doing any preliminary drawings, and the style is that of a "lightning-strike" (Graham-Dixon), making biblical stories look as though they were taking place this very moment. His pictures have a "dangerous unpredictability" to them, are often "metamorphic." The moments of dynamic transformation, or compressed drama, typically come across as minor (and sometimes major) epiphanies. His art is paradoxical, often combining emotions such as awe and unease, or sensitivity and brutality, within a single canvas. Contemporaries were fascinated, bewildered. "Gradually but inexorably," concludes Graham-Dixon, "his dramatic sense of composition...and his sheer rawness of feeling worked themselves into the DNA of Western art" (Rembrandt, Rubens, Vermeer, Manet, Delacroix...), as well as film (Pasolini, Scorsese). Hence the telling remark of the French art critic André Berne-Joffroy, that finally says it all: "What begins in the work of Caravaggio is, quite simply, modern painting."(10)

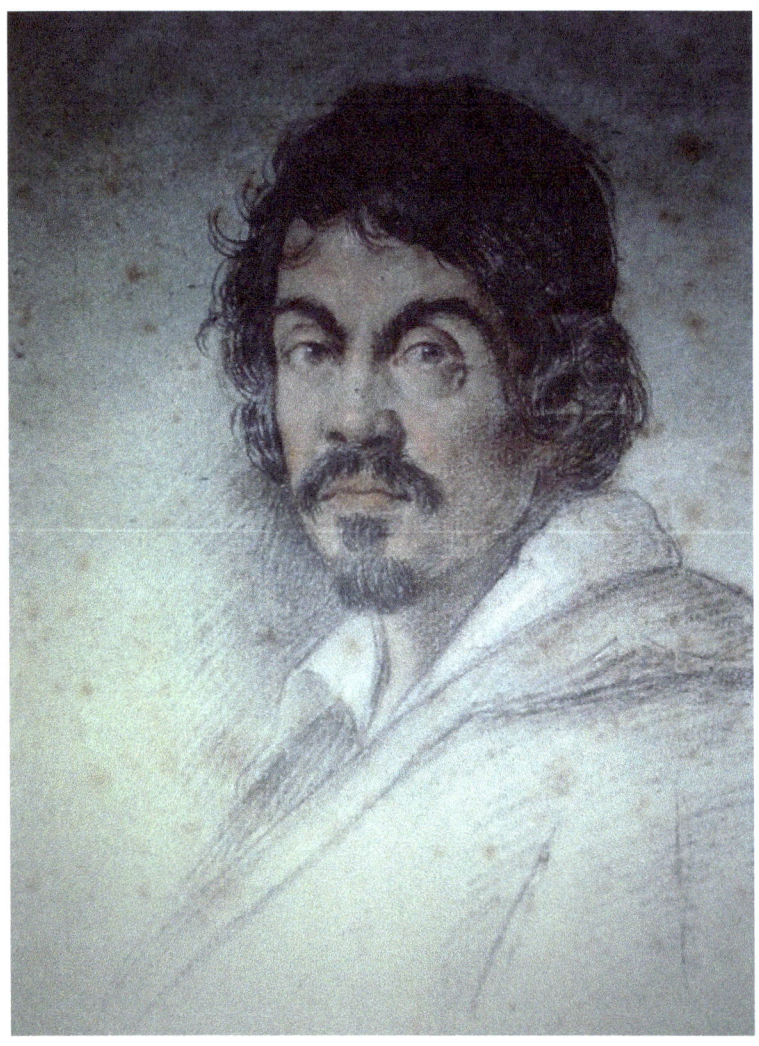

6. Portrait of Caravaggio by Ottavio Leoni

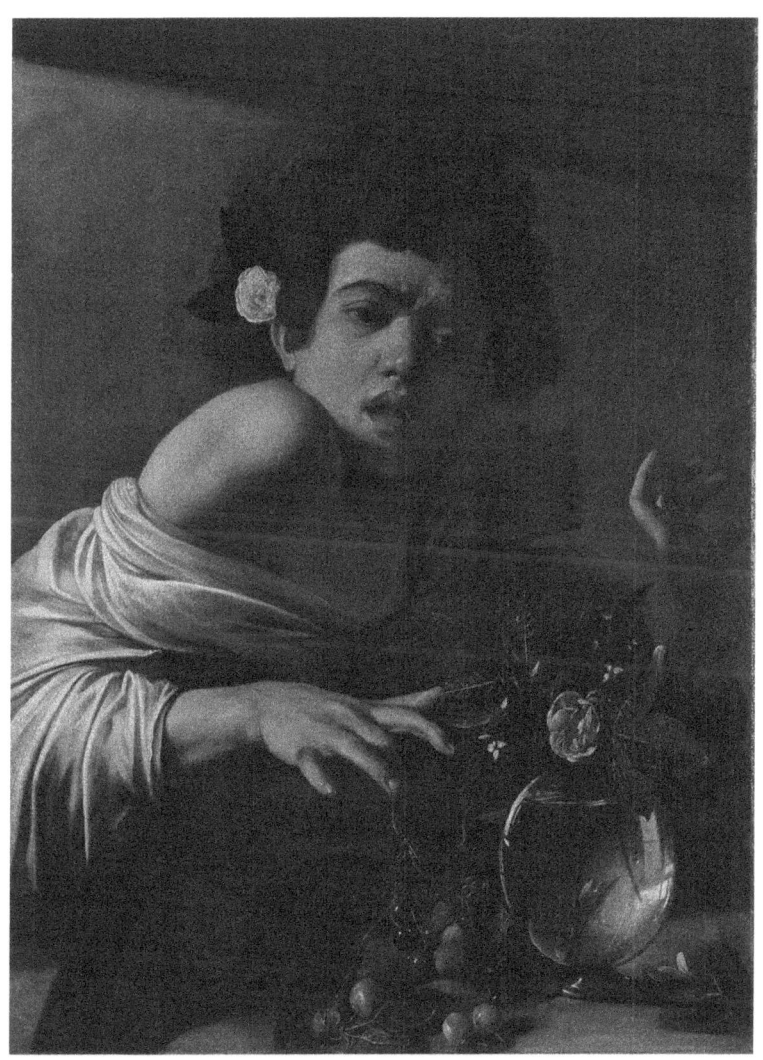

7. *Boy Bitten by a Lizard*

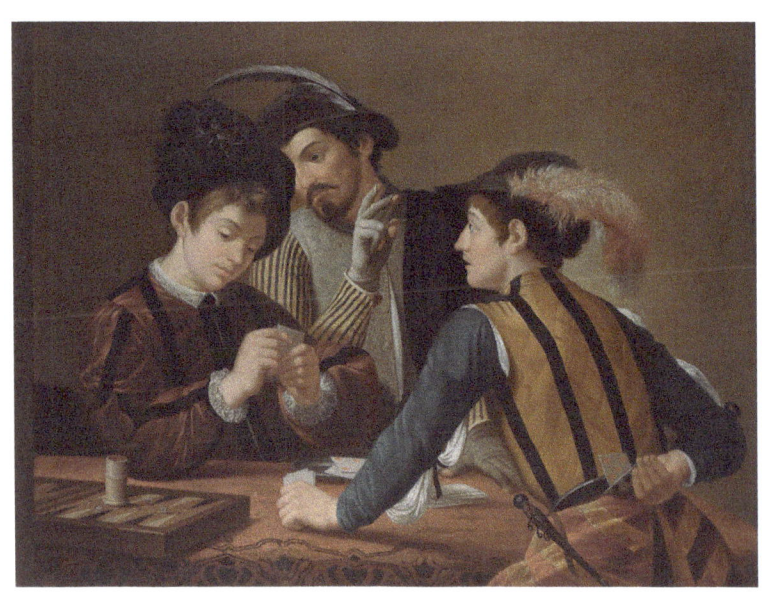

8. The Cardsharps

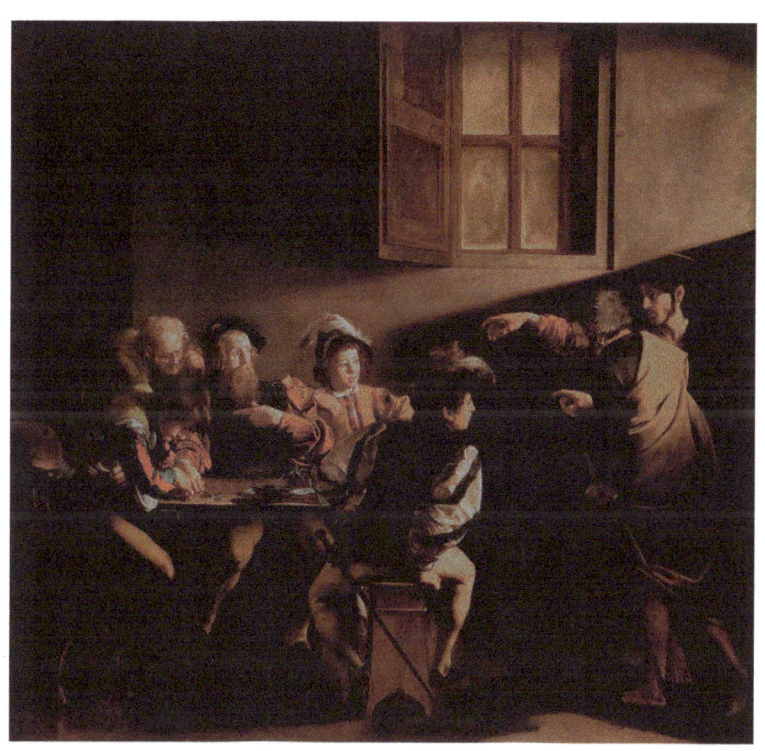

9. The Calling of St. Matthew

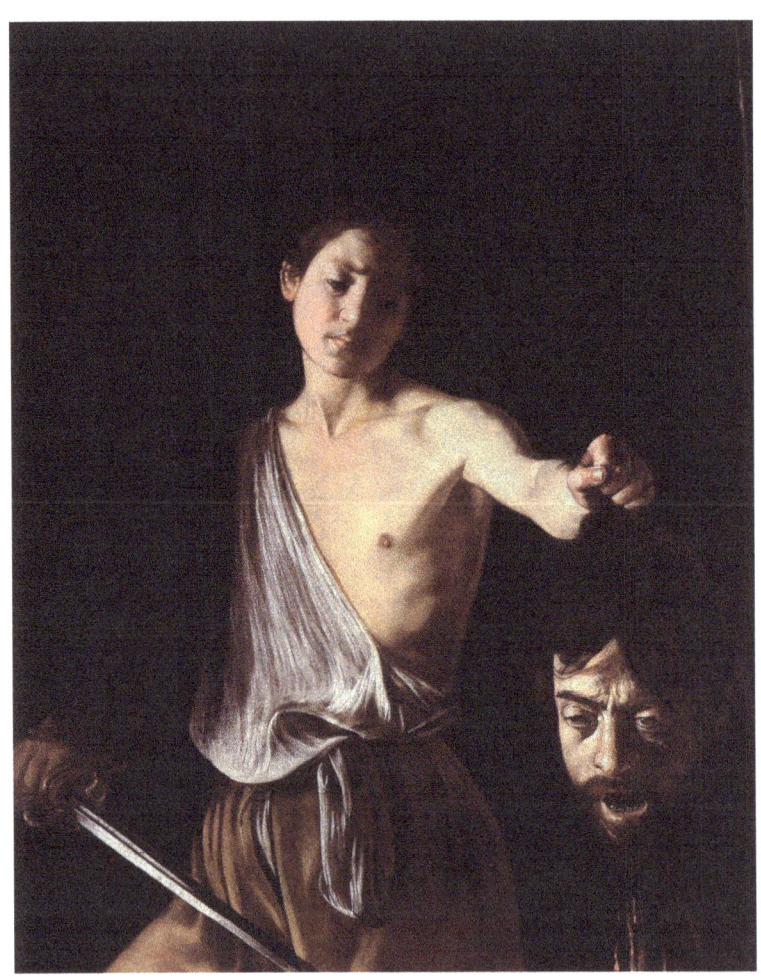

10. David with the Head of Goliath

Three

Fellini: Magic and Pasta

> Life is a combination of magic and pasta.
> —Federico Fellini

> Put yourself into life and never lose your openness, your childish enthusiasm throughout the journey that is life, and things will come your way.
> —Federico Fellini

Movement—*movimento*—could have been Fellini's middle name. Everything about him radiated energy, childish enthusiasm. I have to confess that of all the individuals portrayed in this book, Fellini is the only one with whom I would have gladly exchanged lives. He was not only a great artist, he was also a great teacher. And what he taught—by example—was how to live. Of all the legacies anyone can leave, this is surely the greatest.

Let me start with an overview of Fellini's life (1920-93).(1) He was born in the town of Rimini, in northern Italy, and as a child was an avid reader of popular Italian magazines that reproduced American cartoons. These proved to be an influence on his films, along with American movies by Buster Keaton, Laurel and Hardy, and the Marx Brothers. He also discovered the circus at age six: another formidable influence on his work. In 1938, Fellini decided on a career as a cartoonist and gag writer, and during 1939-42 was on the editorial board of *Marc'Aurelio*, a humor magazine. He married Giulietta Masina in 1943; she would star in a number of his films.

After the Allied liberation of Rome (June 1944), Fellini survived for a while by drawing caricatures of American GIs. Subsequently, Roberto Rossellini hired him to do gags and dialogue for a movie script, and continued working with him afterwards. This was the period of so-called Italian neorealism, when there was a political commitment to portraying postwar poverty and the harsh conditions of Italian life. (*Bicycle Thieves*, by Vittorio De Sica, is probably the most famous film in this genre.) Fellini co-produced and co-directed (with Alberto Lattuada) his first film in 1950, *Variety Lights*, a comedy of sorts set among a group of traveling performers. It proved to be a commercial failure.

Fellini broke with neorealism during 1954-60. *La strada*, possibly his most moving film, an existential meditation on the meaning of life, was released in 1954, and *La dolce vita*, a portrait of the decadence of Roman society, in 1960. *Vita* broke all previous box office records, won the Palme d'Or (highest prize awarded at the Cannes Film Festival), and caused a national uproar for its "immorality." Fellini also met the Jungian analyst Ernst Bernard around this time, which was a major turning point for him. Jung was the single greatest influence on his mature style, marking the definitive move from neorealism to dream-based filmmaking. Freud made us think, wrote Fellini, whereas Jung "allows us to imagine, to dream and to move forward into the dark labyrinth of our being."(2) Several of Jung's major concepts, such as that of the "shadow" and the "anima," made their way into *8½*, among other films.

8½ was released in 1963. In 1962 Fellini had the revelation that the film he was making was about itself, i.e. about the very film he was making. As he described it in later years, "I would make a film telling the story of a director who no longer knows what film he wanted to make." Fellini experimented with LSD in 1964, and later said of his trip: "All I perceived was perception itself....And since the appearance of things was no longer definitive but limitless, this paradisiacal awareness freed me from the reality external to myself." This is a good description of *8½*, as well as a number of other films, such as the hallucinatory *Juliet of the Spirits* (1965). 1973 saw the release of his second-largest commercial success, *Amarcord*, the story of fascism in a small town (like Rimini). It has no plot or linear narrative; Fellini was searching for a "poetic form" of cinema, and seems to have found it.

In 1987, a panel of thirty professionals from eighteen European countries named Fellini the world's greatest director, and *8½* the best European film of all time. In fact, his legacy has been enormous, the inspiration for a great number of films and filmmakers. He died in 1993, having scripted and directed some of the most important films ever made.

There was very little difference, at least in Fellini's mind, between his life and his work. But before we examine his films, let's take a look at his mode of living. It can be summarized in a single word: motion. Fellini was forever on the go, both physically and emotionally. He seemed to inhabit a whirlwind of action. "I love movement around me," he wrote. "That is certainly the main reason why I make films. To me the cinema is an excuse to make things move." Its essential quality, he asserted, was dynamic motion.(3)

Fellini's goal was thus not to make films; it was to move, because for him, movement was equivalent to life. This included movement against fixed forms—fascism, Church dogma, neorealism, Marxism, and so on. "I do not want to have a fixed idea about life," he declared; "I just live." "My system is to have no system," he said on another occasion. "I go to a story to discover what it has to tell me." This explains his attraction to Carl Jung:

"He has allowed us to go through life abandoning ourselves to the lure of mystery." Permanent revolution, unending change, was the way he chose to live his life. This is how he managed to inject a fluid, dynamic quality into our perception of reality; what I have called "space."(4)

For Fellini, in other words, reality was never just one particular thing; he was subversive of *any* order. But one element, one factor, stayed with him throughout his life, and that was his attachment to the world of enchantment—the magical world of the child. As a child, he had paranormal experiences: he imagined he was flying, or living in an alternative universe, for example. Reality for Fellini was not the reality of neorealism. Rather, it was that which had the potential of suddenly becoming magical, or of being seen as magical (which was, for him, the same thing). This connection to childhood enabled him, through his films, to pose two crucial questions: Who are we? Why are we here? He occasionally referred to himself as anti-intellectual, but the fact is that via a visual medium, he emerged as one of the leading intellects of the twentieth century.(5)

Fellini made a total of twenty-four films. As in the case of Bernini and Caravaggio, it will not be necessary to discuss more than a few of his works. Most of them display the quality of "space," or movement, I have been discussing. The films I wish to deal with are the ones generally regarded as his greatest (in addition to *Amarcord*): *La strada, La dolce vita*, and *8½*. Especially in the context of the dominant neorealistic framework, these three amounted to nothing less than a revolution in the art of the cinema. They generated more than "space"; rather, they gave birth to a whole new way of seeing/understanding the world. With *La strada* (*The Road*), Fellini entered into a magical realm, a circus or fantasyland. "The Road" here does not merely represent a physical wandering across Italy; it is more importantly a spiritual journey of self-discovery for both Gelsomina

(Giulietta Masina) and Zampanò (Anthony Quinn). Radical movement in several dimensions, one might say.(6)

It is hard to sit through *La strada* without feeling that your life has been significantly altered. It is equally hard not to be on the verge of tears a good part of the time. The story is, at least on the surface, pretty straightforward. Gelsomina, more child than adult, is a naïve waif who seems to be not quite all there in the head. (Plate 12) She comes from a very poor family, and in order for the family to survive, her mother sells her to Zampanò, to serve as a kind of wife and also as an assistant in his one-man circus act. Her job is to beat a drum and proclaim, "È arrivato Zampanò!" ("Zampanò is here!"). Zampanò is a brute, a man without feelings; his act consists of nothing more complicated than breaking an iron chain by expanding his chest. In the course of their travels, the duo run across the Fool (Richard Basehart), also a circus performer who does a high-wire act on a tightrope. Whereas Zampanò is completely unthinking, living only by force and animal instinct, the Fool is light-hearted, witty, and something of an Existentialist—a clown and philosopher in one.(7)

The transformative moment in the story is known as the "parable of the pebble." Gelsomina is adorable, funny, spontaneous, and creative (Fellini said she was like a cross between a saint and Mickey Mouse!), but ultimately depressed, because she has no sense of any meaning in her life. What exactly is she doing, following Zampanò around the country and beating a drum for this brutish lout who doesn't seem to have any feelings for her? The Fool picks up a pebble and says to her, "Everything has a purpose, even this stone." He convinces her to stay with Zampanò, telling her that this is her purpose. Her depression lifts; she begins to see her connection to Zampanò in a positive light, as part of her destiny. However, there had always been bad blood between Zampanò and the Fool, and in a physical confrontation between them, Zampanò accidentally kills him. After this, Gelsomina becomes slowly unhinged, and can no longer function. The Fool had given her a spiritual vocation, so to speak; with his death, all meaning is lost for her. Zampanò abandons her at the side of the road while she is sleeping; eventually, she curls up and dies. Zampanò learns of her death a few years later, quite by accident, and is haunted, overwhelmed by the news. The film ends with him blindly drunk, lying on a beach, in the sand, crying.

What to make of this? First, we should note that the release of the film provoked a veritable shit storm, especially from Marxists and the neorealist left. *La strada* is actually religious, or mystical; one might say it is a tale of redemption. Fellini had no interest in political correctness or in socioeconomic oppression here; the problems he portrayed are emotional and spiritual. The movie is symbolic, lyrical, and its exact meaning (or message) is deliberately open-ended, ambiguous. It's a kind of fairy tale, really, or parable. Martin Scorsese has said that there is a Franciscan element in the film, for there is compassion not only for Gelsomina and the Fool, but also for Zampanò. The Italian author Italo Calvino wrote that Fellini's visual universe "corresponds to an infantile, disembodied, pre-cinematic visualization of an 'other' world." This was the source of his great creativity. (8)

When *La strada* was awarded the Silver Lion at the Venice Film Festival in 1954, thereby edging out a neorealist film by Luchino Visconti, a fistfight broke out, and a brawl ensued. Years later, Fellini was still astonished by the ferocity of the reaction. He shouldn't have been, because the creation of "space"—and the breach opened up in this case was huge—is always a destabilizing event. This was cinematic poetry. Gelsomina knows nothing about the real world, but like St. Francis, she knows how to communicate with animals. She may, like St.

Francis, be simple, but that is exactly where her strength as a child-woman lies. Many of Fellini's protagonists are individuals whom society would judge as slightly mad, because they are capable of hearing messages from the unconscious, or the natural world. As the film critic André Bazin observed, Gelsomina carries "an aura of the marvelous" around with her.(9)

Second, the film was a huge success; it sold millions of copies. Would-be producers went nuts over it. Walt Disney wanted to turn Gelsomina into an animated cartoon; various producers and directors were hoping to start cranking out sequels, à la *Rocky XV* or *The Karate Kid XXIV*. "I could have lived on Gelsomina for twenty years!" Fellini exclaimed many years later.(10)

Third, *La strada* is a universal insight, an insight into who all of us are, way deep down. This, I believe, is the reaction (recognition) it triggers. It is no accident that in the wake of the film, Giulietta Masina received more than a thousand letters from abandoned women whose husbands subsequently came back to them after seeing it, in addition to letters from people with disabilities, who told her they had gained a new sense of self-worth as a result of seeing the film. *La strada* is also an insight into what Fellini was up to, and he made it explicit. This film, he said, is "the complete catalogue of my entire mythic world." "My films are born not from logic," he went on, "but from love." The film is really the cornerstone of all his work, a fairy tale of his own life. It reveals, says his biographer Tullio Kezich, "the 'reality of the soul' in the face of the vastness of existence."(11)

La strada was the launching pad for Fellini's subsequent work. Film critic Roger Ebert commented that the film was "part of a process of discovery that led to the masterpieces *La Dolce Vita* (1960), *8½* (1963), and *Amarcord* (1974)." Let us, then, turn to *La dolce vita*—"The Good Life."(12)

The story, if so it can be called, consists of a series of disconnected, nonlinear episodes that unfold over a week. Marcello

Rubini, played by Marcello Mastroianni, is a journalist who writes for gossip magazines. During this week, he canvasses Rome's upscale population, the glitterati, searching for love, meaning, and happiness. He finds none of these. What he does find are jaded, superficial people who believe "the good life" is about thrill-seeking, consumerism, and celebrity culture—people like himself, in short. The episodes are empty and depressing, filled with random lovemaking and vapid relationships. This is a new, "modern" morality, created by a booming postwar economy and a mass-consumer lifestyle.(13)

In one episode, two small children claim to have seen the Virgin. Huge crowds, including dozens of paparazzi, gather in a field just outside of Rome to witness this. One mother brings her sick child to be healed; instead, the child is trampled to death in the general melee. In another scene, Marcello meets Steiner, a distinguished intellectual, inside a church playing Bach on the organ. Steiner shows him a book on Sanskrit grammar, to impress him. Later, there is a gathering of intellectuals engaged in pretentious chatter at Steiner's luxurious home. Steiner tells Marcello that he (Steiner) is looking for a more spiritual way of life, and talks about the need for love in the world. Finally, Steiner kills his two children, and then himself. No explanation is given, but the implication is that the life he had created for himself was a bubble, an illusion with no emotional content.

Marcello hopes to become a serious journalist or writer, but by the end of the film he is neither, just a moral degenerate adrift in a society lacking any real values. There is no character development in the movie because there are no genuine characters to develop. The critic Robert Richardson wrote that this was a radically new type of film, one that displayed "an aesthetic of disparity." By the end, he asserted, we see "the disparity between what life has been or could be, and what it actually is." This theme—that of Rome as a moral wasteland—is conveyed not so much by the content of the film (which would be hard to define) as by its visuals, its aesthetic form.(Plate 13)

Movement in the film is constant, partly due to its being so episodic. Much of it is mindless frenzy: the frenetic swarming of the ever-present paparazzi; the endless round of night clubs and all-night parties; the mobs chasing after the children who claimed to have seen the Virgin; people rushing to be saved through money, celebrity, and sex. "The film," writes Tullio Kezich, "is a tragic allegory of the desolation lurking behind the façade of a perpetual carnival." And the making of the film itself was frenetic: daily surprises, constant changes of location, frequent shifting of characters and scenes. It was becoming a Fellini trademark: whirlwind and chaos bordering on complete loss of control. He would decide how to shoot a scene at the last moment, call for new props and set designs, and/or alter the script overnight. Not an easy guy to work with, although no one was really complaining.(14)

Fellini claimed he was not judging or moralizing, that he was merely offering a "comic panorama of life in the fast lane." This is a bit hard to believe. For one thing, the movie certainly isn't funny, except in terms of very dark humor. Fellow director Pier Paolo Pasolini wrote that "it would be hard to imagine a world more completely arid." And the judgment is quite clear: Marcello and everyone around him are spoiled, decadent. Life is portrayed as a farce, a façade. One Fellini biographer, Peter Bondanella, writes that the film is about "public relations stunts, meaningless intellectual debates, empty religious rites, and sterile love affairs." Starlets have replaced priests as status symbols; Christianity no longer has any force, and there is no possibility of redemption here, as there is in *La strada*. The archetypal intellectual (Steiner) proves to be a false prophet; religion, sex, and chic intellectual pursuits don't provide any meaning. To my mind, what Fellini was saying—in a way similar to Marcel Proust—is that we are basically wallowing in bullshit.(15)

Speaking of which, as in the case of *La strada*, the shit once again hit the fan. The film was loudly denounced as immoral; people cursed Fellini, even spat on him. Meanwhile, it broke all previous box-office records, and won dozens of awards. Tickets were quickly selling for 1,000 lire a pop. Although there is something rather boring about it today (all of that frenzied motion finally amounts to nothing), the film is actually quite revolutionary, offering a "lucid self-examination" in terms of how people thought about society and their own lives—or chose not to. Many countries banned it for decades. After all, nearly sixty years later, we are doing exactly the same things depicted in the film, as though it had never been made. One would be hard put, for example, to find a better illustration of the film's razor-sharp portrayal of the supposedly "good life" than contemporary America.(16)

Between *La dolce vita* and *8½*, Fellini began to keep a dream notebook. He wrote down his dreams; he painted them. As a result, his work becomes "primarily oneiric" (Kezich). Life becomes a dream for the maestro; he is no longer interested in reality (conventionally defined). This is signaled by the opening scene of *8½*: film director Guido Anselmi (Marcello Mastroianni), stuck in a traffic jam, is suddenly liberated from it in a surreal sequence in which he floats out of his car and over the city. (Plate 14)(17)

Guido, as it turns out, has lost interest in the sci-fi film he is supposed to be making, and is suffering from "director's block." His crew tries to get him to work on the film, but he evades them. He retreats into a fantasy world, which includes a vignette in which he lords it over a "harem" of women from his (i.e., Fellini's) life. They confront him with harsh truths about his sex life; in a famous scene, he literally whips them into line. Then his Ideal Woman (Claudia Cardinale) arrives, only to tell him that he is incapable of love.(18)

In April 1962 Fellini began writing a letter to his producer, Angelo Rizzoli, saying he had "lost" the film and had to abandon it. But then the chief machinist came in and asked him to celebrate the launch of the film. He stopped writing, went onto the set. Raising a toast to the crew, he felt ashamed. He later wrote: "At that very moment everything fell into place. I got straight to the heart of the film. I would narrate everything that had been happening to me. I would make a film telling the story of a director who no longer knows what film he wanted to make." This was his own transformative moment. Tullio Kezich labeled it "the most sensational confessional in the history of cinema."

As for the film, the rocket ship set from the sci-fi movie is transformed into a circus. Guido directs all of the cast, the people in his life, into a circus ring. They all run around the circle, holding hands, Guido included. He can't do without the people in his life. What he needs to do, in other words, is to accept his life for what it is. The film, in short, is a metafilm: the subject of the film is the making of the film itself, and is also a good example of what Jung referred to as "individuation."

Once again, the production process was characterized by constant motion, endless improvisation. The episodes, even more than in *La dolce vita*, are chaotic, have no relation to one another. The film was often on the verge of falling apart. Guido is always on the move; everything seems to be swirling, including the entire cast of characters at the end in a kind of carousel, or merry-go-round. It's as though Fellini dumped the contents of his unconscious mind onto the screen, without editing them. It's just one big stream of consciousness. Guido/Fellini gains freedom of movement through the power of his imagination. (19)

Life *is* motion, it is "a cabaret, old chum"—and welcome to it. The incoherence, by the end, forms its own type of coherence:

La strada: redemption possible

La dolce vita: redemption not possible

8½: redemption possible through self-acceptance; the carousel at the end is a celebration of one's (messy, fragmented) life as it is

As with the two previous films, *8½* won numerous awards, both within and outside of Italy; once again, it was widely imitated. (One American company even wanted to mass-produce Guido's hat.) Fellini is called a magician, a genius, in the press; one critic wrote that the film "shoved us" into the future. Indeed, many film critics regard it as the greatest film ever made. At the heart of all three of these movies is the question, Why are we here? It's a question that has no easy answer, and which will not go away. If there was ever a filmmaker who got us to think about the meaning of life, it was Federico Fellini.(20)

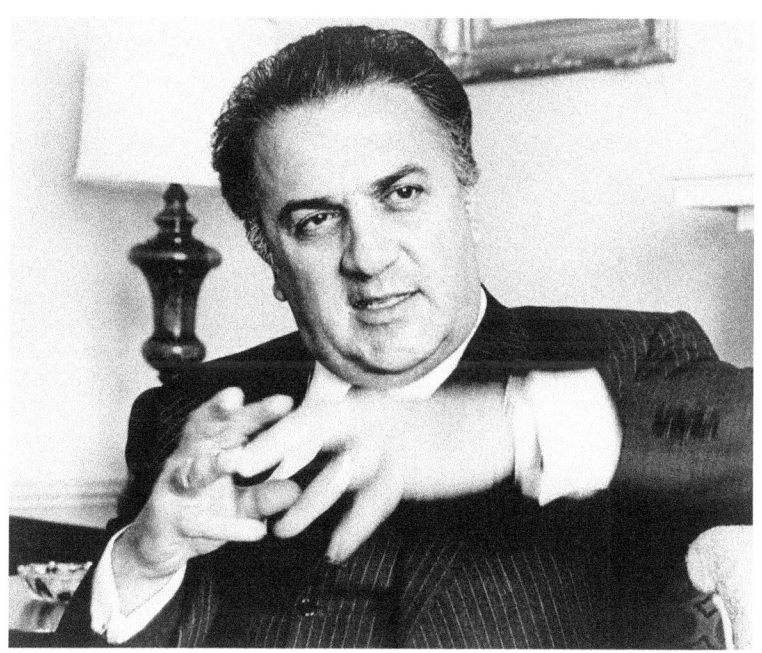

11. Federico Fellini

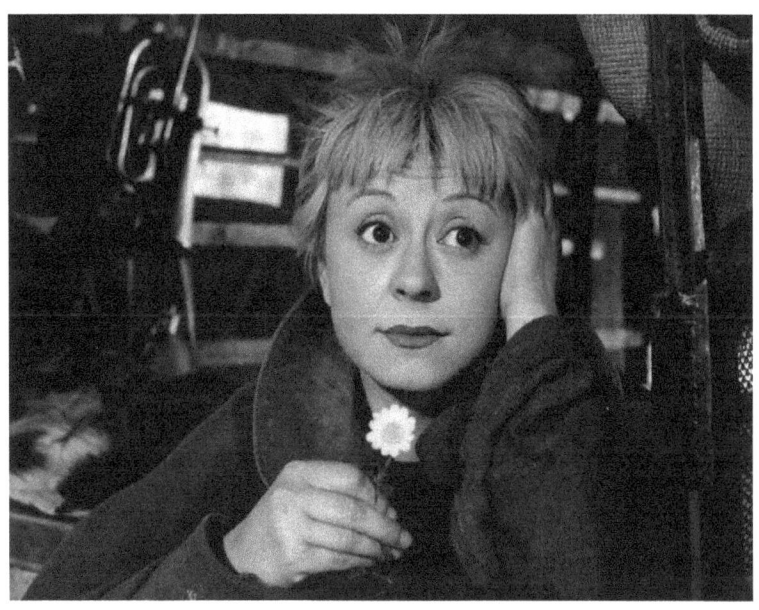

12. Giulietta Masina as Gelsomina in *La strada*

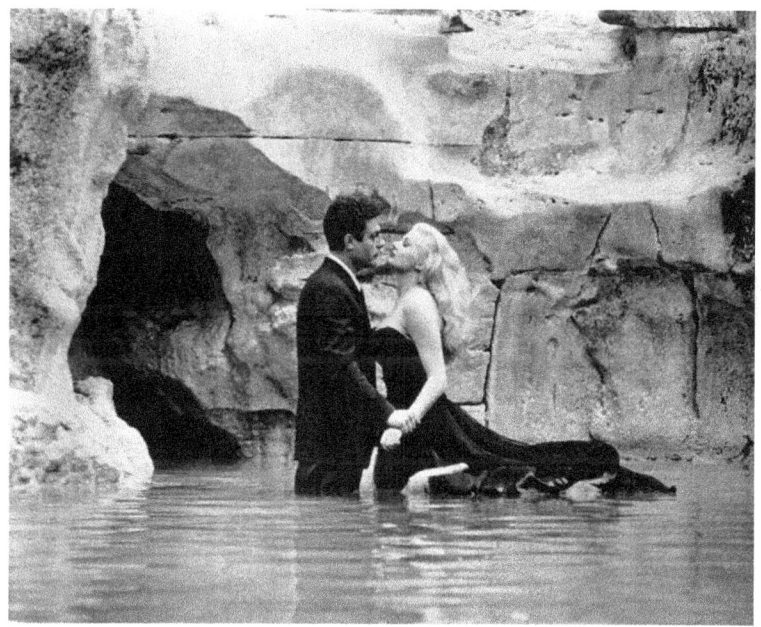

13. Marcello Mastroianni and Anita Ekberg in *La dolce vita*

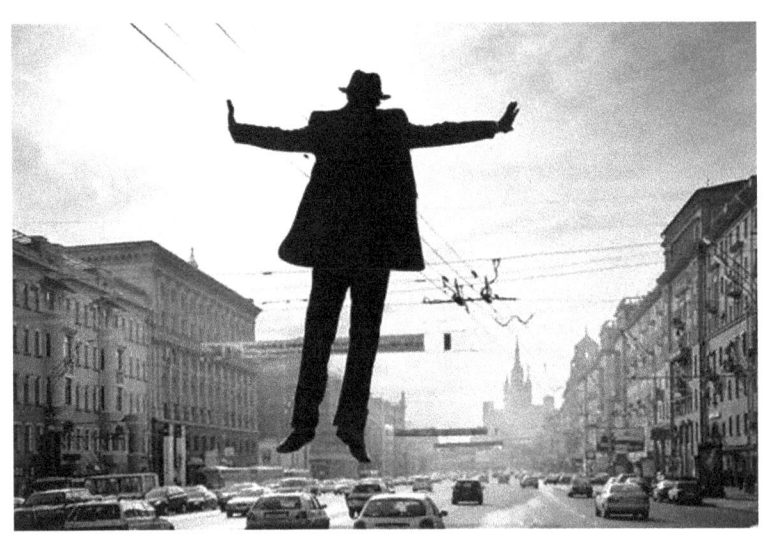

14. Surreal sequence of Marcello Mastroianni in *8½*

Four

St. Francis: A Fool for God

And the Lord told me what He wanted: He wanted me to be a new kind of fool in this world.
—Francis, address to the friars, May 1219

The eager face under the brown hood was that of a man always going somewhere, as if he followed as well as watched the flight of birds. And this sense of motion is indeed the meaning of the whole revolution that he made.
—G.K. Chesterton, *Saint Francis of Assisi*

Attempting to provide a brief sketch of St. Francis' life is a task that borders on the absurd. Francis is, without doubt, everybody's favorite saint, and the collection of books and articles written about him since the thirteenth century could probably fill several large warehouses. What I hope will keep my own account manageable is my focus on the specific themes already discussed: creation of "space"; a break with static contemporary norms; transformation or metamorphosis in the individual and in his work; and the presence of movement in both life and work. Still a tall order, but let's give it a try.(1)

There are many reasons for Francis' immense popularity over the centuries, namely the existence of things in his life and character that speak to practically everyone, regardless of religion or ideological orientation. But there is one particular characteristic that I think is central to the adoration that has lasted for nearly 800 years: an authenticity so blindingly real, that looking at it is comparable to staring directly into the sun. Francis walked his talk. He wanted his life to be an *imitatio Christi*, and he largely succeeded. Not too many in that category, last time I checked.

Of the seven individuals profiled in this book, Francis stands out as being of a different order of magnitude, in terms of greatness, than the rest of them. Of course, a lot of legends have grown up around him that fall into the category of hagiography: that his body broke out in stigmata, or that he arranged a truce with a wolf that was terrorizing the town of Gubbio, and so on. But leaving all that aside, what he accomplished in reality, on the ordinary "street level" of life, so to speak, was nothing short of miraculous. And this extended far beyond his death in 1226, and his canonization in 1228. As I read through various biographies of Francis, I found myself shaking my head in disbelief. How is it possible that such a person even existed?

Francesco di Bernardone was born in Assisi in 1182 (some sources say 1181). His father was a wealthy clothing merchant. As a young man, Francis led a luxurious, carefree life, dressing in expensive clothes and entertaining on a lavish scale. It was an age of a rising middle class; the bourgeoisie was motivated by an obsession with material gain. Accordingly, Francis' goal in life, at this point, was social status and personal achievement. In 1202, at age twenty-one, he joined a military expedition against Perugia. Unfortunately, Perugia won the war, and Francis wound up in prison for a year.

Something changed, as a result. Slowly, back in Assisi, he began to lose his taste for the carefree life. Spiritually speaking, he was adrift. Then one day, sitting in the rundown church of San Damiano, just outside of town, he was looking at the crucifix above the altar when (he later related) Christ spoke to him. "Francis," said the voice, "go and repair My house, which...is falling into ruins." Francis took this instruction literally, i.e. as a reference to that particular church. Looking back over his life, we can see that the message involved something larger: Repair the Christian Church, which had also fallen into ruins.

This event sorted out the confusion in Francis' life; in effect, it rescued him from chaos. He sold some clothing from his father's store and attempted to give the money to the priest of San Damiano. When the latter refused the money, Francis threw it on the ground. His father, however, wanted the money back, and also wanted Francis to forego his inheritance. In the midst of the resulting legal proceedings, Francis stripped naked, gave his clothes to his father, and renounced both him and his patrimony. He would, he said, have only one father from that point on, namely the one who resided in heaven. It was not only a rejection of his father; it was also a repudiation of society's bourgeoning materialism, and the widespread focus on money as the purpose of life.

Francis did rebuild the chapel at San Damiano, along with several other ruined chapels in the nearby countryside. His next transformative moment came when he suddenly, spontaneously, embraced a leper. Lepers, with their peeling skin and disfigured bodies, were the ultimate Other (or "shadow") of Italian society, and everyone was afraid of contagion as well. The embrace was something Francis experienced as a moment of "extraordinary grace." He began to nurse lepers, feed them, wash their bodies. Even beyond the experience of the cross at San Damiano, this was the Great Breakthrough. Honor would henceforth not be found by associating with the elite, the powerful, but with the most despised, the weakest—the outcasts. This, for Francis, was what it meant to follow in the footsteps of Jesus, to lead a true Christian life.

Oddly enough, Francis began to attract followers: eleven of them by 1208. To become a Franciscan, you had to sell everything you owned, give the money to the poor, wear a dirty tunic tied at the waist with a rope, go barefoot, and wander through the countryside preaching a message of peace and love. You had to rebuild churches and tend to lepers. You couldn't store food or save up for the next day.

Movement was central to this way of life, because if you couldn't store anything, you were committed to a life of poverty; which meant you had taken Jesus as your spiritual guide. In a way, the Franciscans were like primitive hunter-gatherers: not storing anything, not engaging in structure or hierarchy, and always being on the move. Francis "was a street person," writes biographer Murray Bodo, "a man of the road...a portable kingdom moving along the streets and roads of the world." "You lived...in constant readiness to move on." By 1216, the number of Franciscans had gone from twelve to more than 3,000.(2)

Let us stop for a moment to consider the meaning of all this. Francis' program was radically new, even revolutionary, in its social context. He offered his followers inner wealth, meaning, and serenity—a more satisfying life, in short, than the endless pursuit of money and status. This was an upside-down world, a way of life based on the refusal of possession. To the world of hustling and opportunism, Francis posed a radically different narrative, namely the poverty of Jesus Christ. People were attracted to the movement because the Franciscans lived what they preached, were obviously touched by grace.

And Francis' preaching was indeed something to behold. He would dance, weep, and make animal sounds. His whole body was constantly in motion. Sometimes he would give a mime performance; at other times, he would take off his clothes. He engaged in gesture a lot, and in a kind of magic ritual. An "indefinable aura" clung to him, according to one biographer, André Vauchez. Vauchez continues: "More than just a sermon, it was a veritable performance during which the body of Francis became the very place where the sacred representation of the Crucified was being played out, a kind of living emblem of Christ." For Francis, God was a kinesthetic experience, one that was tied to our senses. Sounds, smells, sights were all part of it. This was the "crazy wisdom" of Zen masters, or perhaps Sufi saints.(3)

In any event, in 1210 he took his first eleven followers to Rome, to obtain permission from the pope, Innocent III, to found a new religious order. It was good politics, for it was too easy for such a group to be accused of heresy at this point in time. Innocent met with the group, and that night had a dream in which the Church of St. John Lateran (cathedral of Rome, and thus the "home church" of Christendom) began to topple over. At this point, a little beggar leaped from the shadows and supported the building on his shoulders. Innocent awoke, and understood that the beggar was Francis. The symbolism was obvious, and this is in effect what subsequently happened in the real world. Innocent endorsed the Franciscan Order on 16 April 1210, and it became a formal order within the Church in 1223, the Order of Friars Minor.

In 1219 Francis decided to attempt the impossible: he would go to Egypt and try to convert the sultan, al-Kamil, who was a nephew of Saladin's, to Christianity. Ostensibly, this was a perfect way for a Christian to get himself killed. But surprisingly, al-Kamil was willing to let Francis preach to the Muslims in his court. This of course met with no success, but at least he was allowed to leave unharmed. The whole thing was completely unprecedented. Francis was the first person from the West to travel to another continent, let alone a presumably hostile Muslim enclave, with the goal of peacemaking. What looked like a suicide mission turned into a courteous exchange of views, and

Francis was the guest of the sultan for an entire week, after which he caught a boat to Acre and returned to Italy intact. Vauchez remarks that Francis was probably the first Christian saint in the Middle Ages to have made contact with the Muslim world.

Francis' third transformative experience (after the cross at San Damiano and the embrace of the leper) supposedly occurred while he was praying at Mount La Verna (Alverna), in Tuscany, in 1224. According to Brother Leo, a friar who had been with Francis at the time, Francis saw a six-winged angel on a cross, who gave him the stigmata—the five wounds of Christ. How real all this was is still a matter of debate. Since I personally don't believe in stigmata, I have to go with the interpretation of biographer Donald Spoto, who notes that the early accounts of the marks suggest that they could be the results of diseases such as leprosy. Francis himself never claimed that he had received an impression of the wounds of Christ, and never used the word "stigmata"; and the Church itself, in modern times, has stated that there can be physical or psychological explanations for such marks. But in 1224, the event—whatever it was—served to further confirm Francis' reputation as a saint.

As for the impact of the event on Francis himself, Spoto says that in the context of major changes in the Order that were contrary to Francis' original vision, the transformation he subsequently underwent was the ultimate abandonment of his self to God, in "his acceptance of diminishment and pain and in the dissolution of his dreams for his companions."(4) I'll say more about that in a moment. In the meantime, we need to note that the event resulted in the writing of some great poetry, such as the famous *Canticle of Brother Sun* (also known as the *Canticle of the Creatures*). Francis was the first to write poetry in vernacular Italian, so that it could be understood by the common people; and the poem also highlighted his famous ecological sensibility, the notion that nature was the mirror of God. The sun, the moon, the stars, the wind, water—all of these were brothers and sisters, and Francis, as is well known, even preached to the birds.

As the Franciscan membership swelled, problems of structure, management, and politics inevitably arose. Would it really be possible to preserve the original vision in the face of large numbers? As one pope astutely put it, the world was not made only for Franciscans—which is what, in fact, Francis wanted to eventually happen. But lots of friars did not want to have to sleep on the ground, for example, or to be constantly on the move. Given the large membership, these were battles that Francis couldn't win, and he knew it. He had become the classic "inconvenient elder." In 1220 he handed over the governance of the Order to another friar, but he agonized over the shift that was taking place, the primacy of form over content. And in the wake of his death, things hardened even further. Hierarchical levels of privilege emerged; the superiors were allowed to handle money. Posts of responsibility were increasingly seen as ways of enhancing the self, rather than as opportunities to serve. Eventually, the Church did away with the link between the friars and the poor, and was even able to enlist Franciscans in the Crusades and the Inquisition. A number of scholars, including Machiavelli, believed that the Church blew it: Francis gave the papacy three centuries of breathing space, wrote Machiavelli, but the Church failed to take advantage of this, which is why we finally got the Reformation. Its reforms were cosmetic rather than substantive, in short.

Was it all for naught, then? Was Francis just a kind of brilliant comet streaking across the Italian sky, that came and went? Most historians of religion would say no. In the late nineteenth century, one leading historian argued that Francis was "a figure of universal holiness who...belongs to the common patrimony of humanity"—like Gandhi, or Martin Luther King, one might add. It rings true, for whatever the outcome, Francis ushered in a spiritual revolution that has endured as a great ideal, an inspiration to millions. Vauchez believes that the Franciscan movement also contributed to the "feminizing" or "softening" of Christianity that was going on in the thirteenth century, and as such, "constituted a fundamental turning point in the history of Western philosophy." And centuries later, a renewed Catholicism led to the foundation of reformed religious orders—the Theatines, the Capuchins, the Oratorians, the Jesuits, and the Barnabites—dedicated to the Franciscan ideal of poverty. In any case, the Franciscan ideal of authenticity has, *Gott sei Dank*, never really gone away.(5)

What has also lasted over time is Francis' love of animals—his ecological sensibility, mentioned above. It's actually a complex issue, because Francis felt more than one thing about the natural world; it was not all sweet sentimentality and preaching to the birds. His relationship with animals was symbolic as well as concrete, and not always idyllic. But there is enough positive there to affirm that he had a special relationship with the animal kingdom. Around 1220, for example, Francis invented the crèche (Nativity scene), which he displayed in the town of Greccio, near Assisi, at Christmas time. He used real animals, including an ox and a donkey, to create a living tableau, complete with sights and smells. The historian Ernest Renan wrote that "the love and understanding of animals...was greater in him than in any other human being," and Vauchez sees the *Canticle of Brother Sun* as a kind of "mass for the world."(6) We are stewards of the world, on Francis' view; we belong to the world, but we are not its center, and we certainly don't own it. It was not that surprising that Pope John Paul II, in 1979, declared Francis the Patron Saint of Ecology; but in the context of the thirteenth century, all of this was quite amazing.

Let me conclude this chapter with a few words on the issue of movement, to which I have already referred. No less than Bernini, Caravaggio, and Fellini, Francis lived in a kind of whirlwind. Although some biographers do mention this factor of speed in his life, the popular image remains that of a quiet man preaching to birds, rather than that of a man almost constantly on the move. In that sense, the painting by Caravaggio of Francis praying or meditating (Plate 15) is a bit misleading; what we really need is a video of Francis striding across the countryside, or doing one of his body-based sermons before a crowd. And this penchant for movement can be extended to Francis' implied critique of contemporary (i.e., thirteenth-century) Christianity, contemporary money-grubbing, and the contemporary pursuit of power and status. Francis wanted to shake things up, to get people to think about what the good life really is. In addition, movement necessarily meant poverty, and this was the crux of Francis' understanding of Jesus. His whole life reads like a race, wrote G.K. Chesterton; the world was a place to pass through, without settling down. "This sense of motion," Chesterton goes on, "is indeed the meaning of the whole revolution he made."(7) The equation, for Francis, ran something like this: no movement, no poverty; no poverty, no Christ; no Christ, no life. If Francis was a holy man, a fool for God, it was movement that lay at the center of his strange and remarkable success.

In 1952, Roberto Rossellini made a film called *Europa '51*, starring Ingrid Bergman as St. Francis. Fellini wrote much of the script, which argues that the simple faith of the early Franciscans is totally incomprehensible to us today; we can only see it as a form of mental illness. At the end of the movie, Francis is committed to a mental institution. We can only wonder whether it is the Franciscans who were crazy, or a society based on power and profit, which has no real meaning and is going nowhere—like us.(8)

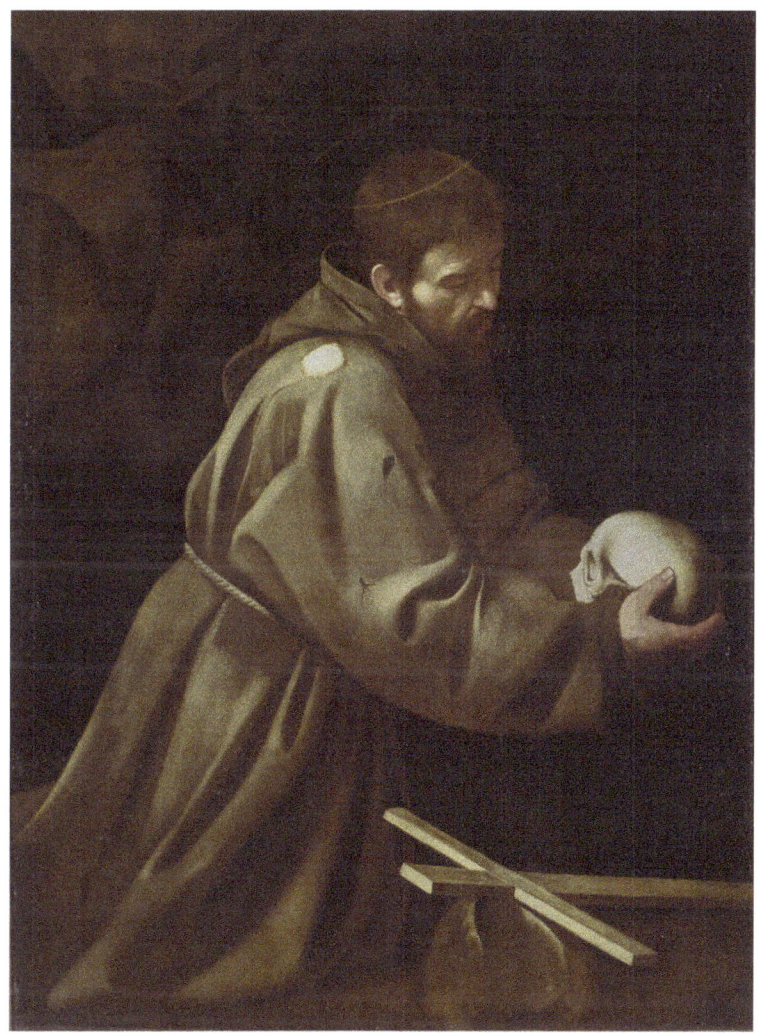

15. Caravaggio, *Saint Francis in Prayer*

Five

Machiavelli: Politics as Science

> It appears to me more proper to go to the real truth of the matter than to its imagination.
> —Machiavelli, *The Prince*

> We are much beholden to Machiavel and others, that write what men [actually] do, and not what they ought to do.
> —Francis Bacon, *The Advancement of Learning*

Of all the individuals surveyed in the present study, Machiavelli is probably the easiest to make the case for transformation, and creating "space." In the fullness of time, his work managed to turn the entire Western political tradition upside down. Indeed, many scholars regard him not merely as the father of modern political theory, but also as the first modern individual *tout court*. However, it is also the case that of all the individuals discussed here, he is the only one who can be characterized as ambiguous, to the point that we are still debating what he actually said (or meant). How else to account for the fact that "Machiavelli studies" is an ongoing industry, and that no less than eight biographies of the man appeared during 2009-17 in the English language alone?

In the popular mind, Machiavelli doesn't have a great reputation. Indeed, he is seen as immoral, when in fact there is an entire school of scholarship that claims that his political theory is more accurately described as *a*moral—neutral, value-free. But the adjective "Machiavellian" conjures up for most of us behavior that is deceitful and manipulative, and it is certainly the case that Machiavelli argued for the frequent need of a ruler to do evil if it were a matter of acquiring or maintaining power. Machiavelli's "New Morality," if so it can be called, was that the end justified the means. We are still living in the shock waves of *The Prince*.

In any case, there are many schools of thought regarding the meaning of his work. Political philosopher Leo Strauss characterized the man as a "teacher of evil," immoral down to his socks. Other scholars, such as Quentin Skinner, see him as a precursor of the modern scientific method, as did Francis Bacon. Personally, I think Strauss may have been right, at least in part, but not for the reasons he advanced. Let me explain.(1)

The crux of Machiavelli's political theory, which flew in the face of classical humanism, was the existential difference between ought and is; what is called, in science and philosophy, the fact-value distinction. Machiavelli was interested in empirical reality: *how* people behaved, not, as in the humanist tradition, how they "should" behave. Thus the eminent philosopher Ernst Cassirer regarded him as the Galileo of politics, separating the facts of political life from moral judgments. On this view, *The Prince* is no more evil than a cookbook, basically a how-to manual for getting and keeping power. As a recent biographer, Miles Unger, puts it:

> As always with Machiavelli, the first consideration—to which all other things were subservient and, in fact, irrelevant—was: What works and what doesn't? The

most elegant solutions on paper were worthless if they did not account for real human passions and feelings, while the most morally repugnant systems should be considered if they improved the average man's lot in life. To this simple and irrefutable logic Machiavelli would cling all his days.(2)

The comparison with Galileo is an apt one, because he too advanced the fact-value distinction roughly 100 years later. To the Inquisition he supposedly declared (rough paraphrase): "Science tells us how the heavens go; it doesn't tell us how to go to heaven." The problem is that as the centuries wore on, science disenchanted the world, as the German sociologist Max Weber put it; it emptied the world of meaning, rendered everything flat, without affect. Add Hiroshima to the equation and by 1945, millions began to regard it as genuinely evil, or at the very least, dangerous. Twenty years later, in the United States and elsewhere, a "counterculture" (especially identified with Herbert Marcuse) had arisen that correctly fingered the problem: there was no such thing as "value-free"; "value-free" was its own type of value. The purported objectivity of science was an illusion, in other words, because its "objectivity" was hardly neutral. The scientific method, and the scientific way of looking at the world, were biased in a particular direction. If science had created "space" in one direction, it severely narrowed it down in another. The human being had become "one-dimensional" (Marcuse), living in an "iron cage" (Weber). None of this would have been possible without Galileo or, for that matter, Machiavelli. (We can throw Bacon and Descartes into the mix as well.)(3)

There is a fair amount of truth to this, but it is not without a certain problem, one that can be seen, for example, in the work of Arthur Koestler. In *The Sleepwalkers*, Koestler saw Galileo as having had a disastrous influence on the course of Western history: "shockingly modern," he called him; a man without a soul. (4) Well, he may, like Machiavelli, have indeed been a modern, way in advance of his time; but I'm not sure that "blame" is the right way to approach these thinkers. It's rather anachronistic to see them entirely through the lens of the American counterculture of the sixties. What Machiavelli and later, Galileo, were doing, was breaking out of the claustrophobic world view of the Middle Ages. If the Scientific Revolution did eventually result in a great deal of evil, which we are living with today, we need to understand that figures such as Machiavelli and Galileo saw what they were doing as expansive, liberatory. When Strauss claims that Machiavelli was *self-consciously* a teacher of evil, that he was a *deliberate* originator of modernity, he is falling into the Koestlerian trap of dubious anachronism. In context, what Machiavelli and Galileo were doing *was* liberatory. The problem is that with the fact-value distinction, and their focus on "how" rather than "why," they sowed the seeds of what would become an enormous headache. Or, to switch metaphors, opened Pandora's box. Over time, amorality became immoral.(5)

The Prince was written in 1513, and published in 1532, five years after Machiavelli's death. It went through twenty-five editions during the next twenty years. The "space" it ultimately generated was that of a freer (more flexible) way of thinking and of operating, of being in the world; and Machiavelli accomplished this by (apparently) rejecting the classical and Florentine humanist tradition *in toto*. The only thing that counts in the political arena, said Machiavelli, was expediency: the ruler needs to see which way the wind is blowing and shift his sails accordingly. Thus it "is necessary for a prince, who wishes to maintain himself, to learn how not to be good, and to use this knowledge and not use it, according to the necessity of the case."(6)

The classical definition of virtue appears in Cicero's most important moral treatise, the *De Officiis* (*On Duties*), which argued that it was only by moral methods that we could achieve our goals. You cannot, said Cicero, be expedient without being morally correct. This way of thinking—that honesty is the best policy—endured through the Renaissance.

Rubbish, said Machiavelli. A prince who follows this path will undermine his own power. Conversely, if a ruler wants to attain his goals, he will not always find it rational or sensible to be moral (virtuous). In fact, Machiavelli goes on, he will *often* be forced to be ruthless, inhumane, for this is the way of the world. Machiavelli's central political axiom was that the key to success lay in recognizing the force of circumstance, and modifying one's behavior to fit the times.(7)

According to Quentin Skinner, the intellectual revolution Machiavelli precipitated was based on inverting the definition of virtue. In the humanist tradition, virtue includes attributes such as honesty, fairness, decency, and so on, and especially, a willingness to put the public good before private interests. On the contrary, said Machiavelli; the defining characteristic of a virtuoso prince is a willingness to do whatever it takes to get the job done—even if the action is wicked, even if it entails force or fraud. He gives the example of Cesare Borgia, whose brutality allowed him to stay in power (for a while, anyway). Borgia was cruel, but this enabled him to restore order to the Romagna. Machiavelli admires this, and urges other rulers to follow in his footsteps. "It is much safer to be feared than loved," he wrote, in what Skinner calls a "scornful rejection of conventional humanist morality."

This is indeed modern; it is exactly how politics works in the modern world. The worst injustices, including torture and the massacre of innocents, are committed by governments that invoke "national security" as a catch-all smoke screen to allow them to do whatever they want. If this is the famous Machiavellian "flexibility," or amorality, we would surely be better off without it. And those very few who refuse to play the game—whistleblowers and other individuals with a conscience, who prefer principles to power—typically have their lives destroyed or at the very least, are marginalized and rendered irrelevant. Machiavelli himself admits this. Most people, he says, are vulgar—by which he means willing to play the game, or easily be seduced by it. Those few who aren't, he adds, are isolated.(8)

So we need to ask: Machiavelli did indeed open up a lot of "space" in our modes of thinking and behaving, but is it a space we (who "we" is, of course unclear) wish to inhabit? The problem with space and transformation and even genius is that they really *are* value-neutral: you don't necessarily get a Fellini or a Francis every time these things show up. Indeed, you might even get a fascist (see Ch. 7). I regard Machiavelli (or someone like him) as inevitable, historically speaking; but his legacy is something like the proverbial bone stuck in your throat that you can't swallow, but also can't throw up. The bone may get dissolved with the passing of modernity, but for all the hip talk about a postmodern age, we are hardly there yet. In a way, *The Prince* is like those sex manuals that were popular in the sixties: the techniques are clear, but there seems to be a strange absence of love.

Well, that's one side of the argument. It may be unfair. Was Machiavelli really all "how," and no "why"? Was there no larger purpose to his political agenda other than power for its own sake? In *Thoughts on Machiavelli*, Strauss asserts that Machiavelli "has no sense of the sacredness of 'the common'." But it turns out that Machiavelli wrote more than one book, and it is here that a third school of thought emerges, the "republican" interpretation (see n.1). For another book, considered by many scholars to be far superior to *The Prince*, is the *Discourses*, written in 1517 and published in 1531. (Full title: *Discourses on the First Ten Books of Titus Livy*) In this work, Machiavelli does talk in terms of "ought." He comes out in favor of republics, and discusses how a republic *should* be structured. As for the advantages of the latter: "The governments of the people are better than those of princes," he writes; "If we compare the faults of a people with those of princes, as well as their respective good qualities, we shall find the people vastly superior in all that is good and glorious."(9)

And there is more along these lines. In 1519, Pope Leo X, a member of the Medici family, decided that he wanted input from experts on reforming the government of Florence. In response, Machiavelli submitted a proposal for this in 1520, a *Discourse on the Remodeling of the Government of Florence*, in which he argued that if the Medici wished to secure or maintain their political power, they would have to act to promote the common good; and that the key to that was equality: fairer distribution of wealth, more widely shared power, and equal treatment under the law (ideas that also appear in the *Discourses*). Of course, the Medici had no interest in any of that. Machiavelli never got a hearing, and the non-republican, princely government of Florence only got worse as time went on. But it is noteworthy that Machiavelli took a stand, in his *Discourse*, for "ought," for the imagination—not just for what is; that he was not "just" a scientist. In the past, he pointed out, great thinkers—Plato and Aristotle, for example—when unable to form a republic in reality, did so in their imaginations, in writing. Hey, at least it's something, he seemed to be saying.(10)

Which is why I stated earlier that Machiavelli is one of the most ambiguous figures around. For example, despite his clear preference for republican regimes over princely ones, Machiavelli reaffirms the idea (in the *Discourses*) that virtue means doing whatever is necessary to obtain civic glory. "The story of his life," writes historian Hans Baron, "will always have to be presented as a delicate texture of sometimes contrasting motivations."(11)

Machiavelli is not only an ambiguous figure; he is also a frustrating one. I have a feeling that Leo Strauss hated him precisely because he was right: men are driven by a lust for power and glory and will do whatever is necessary to obtain them. In the war between conscience and self-aggrandizement, the latter wins out more than 99 percent of the time. For millions around the world, the political struggle of our time, in their minds, is that of Left vs. Right; the problem is that neither camp has a monopoly on virtuous behavior, and both sides are predictably unscrupulous if it is to their advantage to be so. Machiavelli was hardly deluded on that score. As a result, I believe that he perceived a deeper and much more important struggle, one that might be characterized as the conflict between ego and decency. From early on, Machiavelli's defenders argued that beyond expediency, his real goal was to uphold high moral standards, an argument reiterated by the Italian philosopher Benedetto Croce nearly 400 years later. Machiavelli fully recognized that we live, for the most part, in the world of ego; of power and manipulation, in short. This was the hard truth of the matter. But what he wanted was that we shift our priorities—really, our entire way of life—and live instead in a world of decency, of fairness. All he was finally able to do in that direction was sketch out what that might look like; it is hardly an accident that he admired St. Francis. I suspect that he understood that until we could make that crucial shift, the common good would never be more than an elusive ideal, a "beatific vision" (Isaiah Berlin) shimmering on the horizon. No wonder he was, according to Croce, "one of the loftiest and most sorrowful souls" in all of human history. (12)

One more possibility, before we move on (or back) to the twentieth century. If "high moral standards" include candor and honesty, then we need to note that Machiavelli did not follow his counsel to princes that they be crafty and deceitful whenever it served to advance their interests, in his own life. "Machiavelli himself," writes Miles Unger, "was the least Machiavellian of men." His behavior was characterized by candor and sincerity (which often got him into trouble); the "lack of guile in his own life stands out in contrast" to what he was telling rulers to do. This would seem to confirm the notion that for him, the crucial categories of human existence were ultimately not this or that political position, but rather ego vs. decency. This was, in other words, the bottom line beneath the bottom line, because how he personally conducted his life must surely tell us something about what he actually believed.(13)

Regardless of how one chooses to see Machiavelli, there is no question that his legacy has been enormous. Many twentieth-century critics regard him as the first modern man, although one might argue that like the medieval St. Francis, he was asking us to think deeply as to what our lives are finally all about, or should be about. Autocrats, of course, were fascinated with him, including Henry VIII, Mussolini, and Stalin. As stated earlier, Francis Bacon saw him as a precursor of modern science, and he was also an influence on Spinoza, Rousseau, Edward Gibbon, and Adam Smith. Some scholars have argued that he had a major impact on America's Founding Fathers, John Adams in particular (the idea of mixed government); and Franklin, Madison, and Jefferson all admired his republican sentiments. Finally, as we shall see in Ch. 6, he was certainly an inspiration for Antonio Gramsci's brand of socialism. Paraphrasing Milton Friedman on John Maynard Keynes, one might summarize it this way: "We are all Machiavellians now."(14)

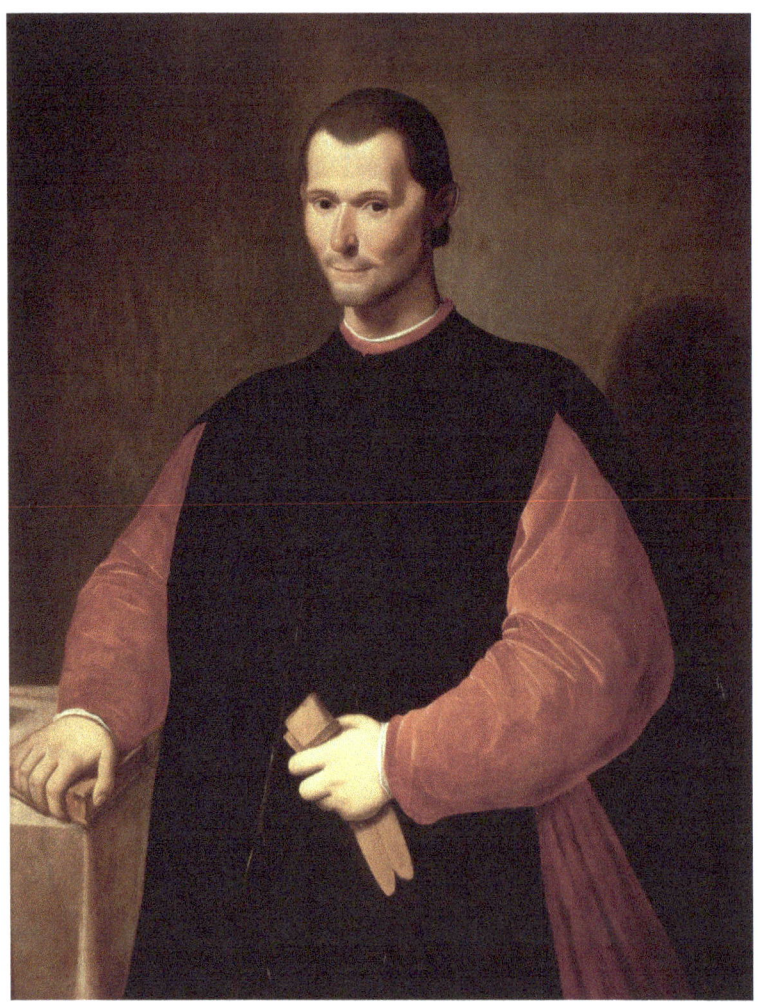

16. Portrait of Machiavelli by Santi di Tito

Six

Gramsci: Mind over Matter

In the social production which men carry on they enter into definite relations that are indispensible and independent of their will; these relations of production correspond to a definite stage of development of their material powers of production. The sum total of these relations of production constitutes the economic structure of society—the real foundation, on which rise legal and political superstructures and to which correspond definite forms of social consciousness. The mode of production in material life determines the general character of the social, political, and spiritual processes of life. It is not the consciousness of men that determines their existence, but, on the contrary, their social existence determines their consciousness.
—Karl Marx, *A Contribution to the Critique of Political Economy*

Man is above all else mind, consciousness...
—Antonio Gramsci

As in the case of St. Francis and Machiavelli, trying to present a "snapshot" of Gramsci is a rather daunting task. Once again, the literature is quite vast, especially in Italian, as the man is a national hero. But there is an additional complication with Gramsci, in that his thought is not systematic and is typically fragmentary, due to the fact that the bulk of his work—thirty-two notebooks amounting to nearly 3,000 pages—was written in a fascist prison, where he spent ten years of his life and ultimately died in 1937, at age forty-six. Physically speaking, his life was one of almost unrelieved physical and emotional suffering, which also didn't help. He was a hunchback, very short in stature, and had to endure extreme poverty for much of his life. He was, in a word, a most unlikely candidate for opening a huge "space" in Marxist theory and sociology in general, such that eighty years after his death, Gramscian analysis is actively being applied to political theory, history, cultural studies, and related fields.(1)

It is possible, given the failure of Marxism, that the reader might be wondering why I chose to bother with a Marxist scholar at all. By "failure," I mean that Marx's prediction of a proletarian revolution in the industrial nations never materialized, and in addition, the communist regime of the Soviet Union completely imploded. As it turns out, Gramsci's version of Marxism is able to explain these failures; and if Marx's predictive powers proved to be rather weak, his analytical powers, at least in the case of capitalism, were outstanding. Much of *The Communist Manifesto*, published in 1848, reads like it could have been written yesterday. When Marx and Engels observe that capitalism "has left remaining no other nexus between man and man than naked self-interest," and has drowned every human emotion "in the icy water of egotistical calculation," they are describing neoliberalism in general and the United States in particular (in neon, one might even say). Analytically speaking, this is no musty, fuddy-duddy theory that needs to be mothballed. On the contrary: after 170 years, it still has much to teach us.(2)

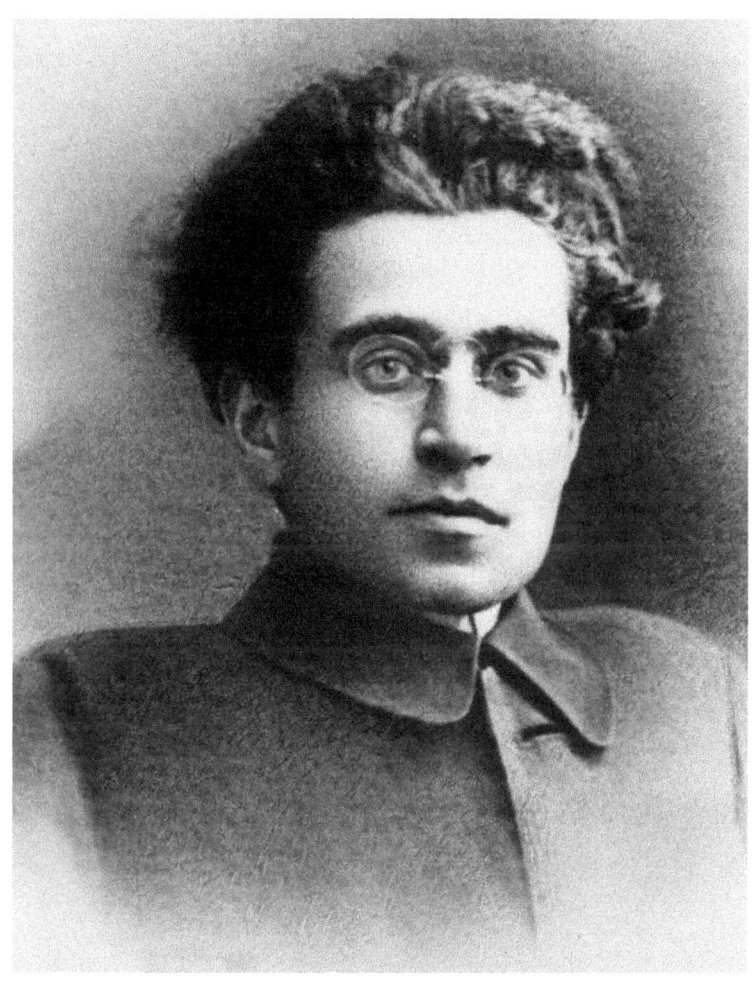

17. Antonio Gramsci

Gramsci's key concept, the one that broke with strict Marxist economic determinism and thereby provided a much larger understanding of social process, is known as "hegemony" (*egemonia*). Before we can unpack the term, however, it will be necessary to say a few words about orthodox Marxist theory, to which Gramsci was reacting.

As the above epigraph from Marx would indicate, Marx saw the activities of men and society operating on two hierarchical levels, which he called "base" and "superstructure." The base was the economic reality, the so-called mode of production. Built upon that was the superstructure, namely the phenomena of the human mind: ideas, ideologies, religions, and what in general we refer to as culture. The key point here is that the latter is a product of the former, is in fact determined by it. An analogy might be a locomotive: the coal and the engine at the bottom (the economy) generate the steam that comes out at the top (culture). In addition, the ideas of any age correspond to the mode of production dominant in that age. A feudal society based on land and agricultural labor (slaves and serfs) has one set of beliefs; a capitalist society based on industry and manufacturing has a very different set of beliefs. There is a tendency, said Marx, for the members of any society, any era, to regard their beliefs as eternal, valid for all times and places; but just let the mode of production change, and all of those "certainties" fly out the window, to be replaced by new ones. Ideas, in a word, are fluff:

> The phantoms formed in the human brain are also, necessarily, sublimates of their material life processes, which is empirically verifiable and bound to material premises. Morality, religion, metaphysics, all the rest of ideology and their corresponding forms of consciousness, thus no longer retain the semblance of independence.(3)

And in fact, it gets worse, because the superstructure is not merely fluff reflected off of the base, but constitutes a con game that draws the whole of society into itself. "The ruling ideas of each age," write Marx and Engels, "have ever been the ideas of its ruling class." In his biography of Marx, Isaiah Berlin says that what Marx meant by this was that in capitalist societies, the majority "work for the benefit, and according to the ideas of others...their ideas and ideals correspond not to their own real predicament...but to the aims of their oppressors. Hence their lives rest on a lie." The purpose of the superstructure, as far as the ruling class is concerned, is to justify its own privileged status, and this it does by getting the rest of society to regard its values as eternal, part of the natural order of things. This thesis was also asserted by Erich Fromm in *Escape from Freedom* (1941), and more recently by Nicole Aschoff in *The New Prophets of Capital*:

> For capitalism to survive and thrive, people must willingly participate in and reproduce its structures and norms....Large swathes of the population must actively, or at least passively, believe that capitalist society is worth their creativity, energy, and passion, that it will provide a sense of meaning, that it meets their need for justice and security.(4)

The carrot is more effective than the stick, in short; we have now arrived at the threshold of Gramsci's "hegemony."

As already noted, Marx's prediction of inevitable proletarian revolution in the nations of Western Europe did not pan out, and in addition, the Russian Revolution didn't fit the mold. Marxism had it that the evolution to a communist society had to follow a strict progression of economic stages, and here Russia had gone from quasi-feudalism to communism without the intervening stage of capitalism. Gramsci realized that Marx's economic determinism was too mechanical a formula to be true to life, and that in particular, the superstructure had been given short shrift. *Ideas mattered*, in a word; the superstructure was not just the economy's country cousin, or bastard child. This realization opened up a tremendous transformative space in the field of social and political analysis, because the task now was to figure out what sort of power (hegemony) the superstructure had, and how it interacted with the base. This "second-stage Marxism" was Gramsci's gift to the world.(5)

In any case: hegemony. Gramscian analysts have tended to explain it better than Gramsci, oddly enough. Here is the Welsh historian Gwyn Williams:

> An order in which a certain way of life and thought is dominant, in which one concept of reality is diffused throughout society in all its institutional and private manifestations, informing with its spirit all taste, morality, customs, religious and political principles, and all social relations, particularly in their intellectual and moral connotation.(6)

This represents persuasive, as opposed to coercive, power; an idea that Gramsci originally got (in part) from Machiavelli. In Chapter 18 of *The Prince*, Machiavelli evokes the mythological image of the centaur, half-human half-beast, and says that "there are two methods of fighting, the one by law, the other by force." A prince, he continues, must be able to employ both methods, because in terms of wielding or retaining power, "the one without the other is not durable." Velvet glove, iron fist.(7)

If governance or power requires a balance between law and force, consent and coercion, then persuasion, by means of hegemony (which could be mostly unconscious), is the normal form of social control. The system, in short, is never questioned except by a few beatniks like Allen Ginsberg ("Howl"). But if the "counter-hegemonic vision" of these marginal folks begins to attract a serious following, then the velvet gloves come off: protesters are beaten by the police, or even shot at Kent State. The ruling class will make nice so long as it doesn't feel its hegemony is threatened. If, on the other hand, the system goes into crisis mode, the Power Elite (C. Wright Mills) bares its teeth; which were there all along. From Huxley (*Brave New World*) to Orwell (*1984*), in other words.(8)

The crisis, of course, is a spiritual-intellectual one: large numbers of people come to question the "common sense" of the hegemonic regime (what Mills referred to as "crackpot realism") —which might be, for example, the values and world view of capitalism—and feel they've been sold a bill of goods. I'm working fourteen hours a day for what, exactly? And if an alternative way of life presents itself, in particular with the possibility of replacing the current hegemonic pattern with a different one, then what you have is a crisis of faith, and potentially, of power.

It might help to further our understanding of Gramscian political analysis if we were to take a closer look at hegemony. For Gramsci, capitalism was not just economics; rather, it was a whole way of life. Culture, he believed, was the site of political struggles. The terrain of this fight was what he called "civil society"—institutions such as the church, unions, the press, museums, and so on. The hegemony of the ruling class is expressed through institutions such as these; it uses them to reinforce its view of the world, and the rest of the population passively absorbs this view without much reflection—i.e., sees it as ethical and universal. The system is relatively stable because the "subaltern" (lower, excluded) classes buy into it, identify with the dominant (hegemonic) value system. This—government by consent, with coercion lurking in the background—might be termed a successful regime. The most stable regime, Gramsci believed, was one in which the coercion was the least visible.(9)

This raises the issue of "false consciousness"—Noam Chomsky's idea of "manufactured consent." How should a revolutionary political party, or a group of beatniks or hippies, approach the 99 percent of the population who are not in the ruling class? Should it tell them that they've been brainwashed, that their values are misplaced, and that they really *don't* (*pace* Janis Joplin) want a Mercedes Benz? And if they were to reply—as they did—"No, I *do* want a Mercedes Benz"—what then? The point is that very few social orders can be described as a conspiracy of evil rulers. I'll return to this issue of counter-hegemony in a moment.

Politics, wrote Gramsci, can transcend economics, bring into play motives beyond that of profit—such as emotions and aspirations. It is relatively autonomous, then, not mechanically tied to an economic base.(10) "Liberals" in America have endlessly puzzled over the question of why the lower classes vote against their own interests, when the answer is quite clear: their interests are not just, or even primarily, economic. They are also hegemonic, which is to say cultural and symbolic. The working class is embarrassed by welfare payments because the hegemonic ideal is that of rugged individualism. It may not share the liberal program of taking down Confederate statues. It supports America's foreign wars because that is the patriotic thing to do, even when it is its children who die in them. Etc. And in particular, it retains a shred of self-respect: it doesn't want to be told what to do, or how to live. It (incorrectly) sees its world view as self-generated, even unique.

For Gramsci, analyzing how hegemony operates was not just some academic exercise. He agreed with Marx that studying the world was fine, but that the point was to change it. This is where the notion of counter-hegemony comes into play. If the fight takes place on the ideological or perceptual terrain, then the job of the hegemonic intellectuals—whom Gramsci designated as "traditional" intellectuals—is to serve the ruling class by toeing the line, so to speak. In Gramsci's day (and probably today as well) it included writers for the *Corriere della Sera* and *La Stampa*; in the United States, journalists associated with the *Washington Post* and the *New York Times* fall into this category. Their job is to reassure the professional middle and upper-middle classes that despite the obvious chaos and dysfunction in which the nation finds itself, you needn't worry: ultimately, all is well. (I used to tell my classes that given the topic, I could write the perfect *Wall Street Journal* editorial blindfolded.) Most university professors fall into this category: the state has been good to them, economically speaking, so they are not about to rock the boat.(11)

The other type of intellectuals—intellectuals-in-the-making, we would have to say—Gramsci called "organic." These are the leaders who need to educate the working class about hegemony in general, the situation they are in, and the fact that there is a socialist, counter-hegemonic alternative that can potentially free them from their oppression. The goal is to get the workers to a point of self-conscious awareness; to recognize themselves as a class. To that end, Gramsci put a lot of emphasis on education; and when he was able to, he traveled around the country giving classes and lectures on Marxism and related topics. This was, in his words, a "civilizing mission." His favorite example of this cultural process was the French Enlightenment, the *philosophes* like Voltaire and Rousseau, who paved the way for the French Revolution through the power and distribution of counter-hegemonic ideas.

However, "leaders" is not a word Gramsci used in the traditional sense. He believed that these intellectuals did have to be fully organic—i.e., arise from the people; that subaltern groups had to develop their own spokesmen and women. He also saw this type of "awakening" as psychological, even epiphanic: that individual members of the working class must achieve this self-consciousness through moments of self-recognition. He called this process "catharsis," and said that these were moments of rare intensity. Once this larger realization spread through the proletariat, the latter would be en route to revolution.(12)

Of course, it didn't work out that way, as we all know. Gramsci was struck by the apparent indifference of the masses to socialism or revolution, and he gave as one explanation of this the fact that the dominant hegemonic paradigm was so powerful. The workers were immersed in it, and simply couldn't see beyond it.(13) It could also be argued that socialism didn't speak to them; that they weren't terribly interested in it, and in any event found it abstract, even impenetrable. I recall a discussion I had in the seventies with an environmental activist in San Francisco, who told me: "During the sixties we kept looking for a welder or carpenter who read Sartre or Marx. We never found him." Still, all is not lost: the work of Gramsci and the concept of hegemony can be used to illuminate the nature, the workings, of entire societies, with greater flexibility and insight than Marxist determinism could ever do. Let me take the United States as an example.

The hegemonic paradigm of the United States is known as the American Dream. It is a mythology that has a number of aspects to it, but perhaps the most important of these is the notion of growth—unlimited economic and technological expansion. Almost every American is engaged in this project, as Alexis de Tocqueville observed nearly 200 years ago; I have referred to it elsewhere as "hustling." The idea is to carve out a space for oneself, especially along economic lines, and then keep enlarging it. Conspicuous consumption (Thorstein Veblen) and consumerism in general are its most obvious expressions. On a national scale, it was the motive behind the Manifest Destiny of the nineteenth century, and of most of our (imperial) wars.(14)

The American Dream is kept alive by many sources; success is literally a religion in the U.S. Without it as a goal, most Americans would be lost. We are inundated by Horatio Alger-type stories, celebrity culture, TV commercials, and endless corporate propaganda that admires those individuals worth billions of dollars. That such people may be sleazy, dishonest, and cruel is of no consequence to most Americans. Asked, some years ago, about their attitudes to the upper 1 percent (this was a poll taken by the Pew Charitable Trust), most Americans indicated that their goal was to enter their ranks. The poor, who are hurt the most by this ideology and way of life, turn out to be its staunchest defenders, and are intensely patriotic. And in my own experience, if one should suggest to an American that this way of life is spiritually empty, or that the earth doesn't possess infinite resources, the typical reaction is frequently one of red-faced rage, accompanied by the shouting of (hegemonic) slogans. "Growth" is the real American religion, then—"our golden calf," as the economist Herman Daly once put it.(15)

The seventies in the United States proved to be very unusual in this regard, because those years saw the emergence of a counter-hegemonic ideology. The individual most identified with this latter, in both a spiritual and ecological sense, was President Jimmy Carter, in office during 1977-80; but what got the ball rolling was the famous/notorious *Limits to Growth* study, published in 1972 by the Club of Rome. The study was computer-generated and data-rich; its message was that if we kept to our trajectory of limitless expansion, there would be hell to pay: a wholesale systems crash, the collapse of civilization.(16)

Reaction to the study was not unlike the one I described above, my "conversation" with a typical American; and when you get a heated, emotional reaction, it's usually because your interlocutor is terrified that you might be right. The Israelites were not at all happy with Moses' decision to burn the golden calf and substitute for it a set of rules limiting their behavior. This is pretty much what happened, metaphorically speaking, in the wake of the publication of *Limits to Growth*. As journalist Christopher Ketcham tells us, the study was the subject of an immediate, and vicious, attack. A *New York Times* article by three economics professors called it "pseudoscience," "polemical fiction," a piece of "technical chicanery." Review after review displayed an evangelical fervor in suggesting that the book be summarily dismissed, using phrases such as "an impudent piece of nonsense." It was a clear assault on the American Dream; Americans were correspondingly outraged. President Reagan, of course, hated it, assuring his audiences (years later) that there were "no such things as limits to growth."

Well, who had the last laugh? In 2016, a British parliamentary group reported that the 1972 predictions were basically correct. Several ecologists came to the same conclusion, and one major investment banker declared (this in 2000) that the *Limits* study was amazing, in the sense of how accurate its extrapolations had proven to be. The thirty-year update of the original study, released in 2004, observed that the warnings provided in the original book had been ignored ("vilified" would be more accurate), and that we were likely headed for disaster as a result. (17)

What all this has to do with hegemony should be fairly obvious, especially when we translate the debate to the arena of national politics. As suggested above, Jimmy Carter broke with the American Dream. He was aware of the *Limits* study, along with numerous texts that preceded his move to the White House in 1977: *Small Is Beautiful*, by E.F. Schumacher, for example, along with works by Barry Commoner, William Ophuls, Wendell Berry et al. All of this saturated the air of the seventies, including notions of voluntary simplicity, steady-state economy, appropriate technology, and so on. Progress for its own sake—the American Dream, in short—was coming under heavy scrutiny. This was a counter-hegemonic tradition, then, suggesting that we start living a different way, a way characterized by austerity, restraint, and sustainability. You couldn't get more un-American than this. Looking back, it seems amazing that such a discussion could even happen in the United States, let alone last for nearly a decade. Jimmy cultivated a "plain style" (still does). He invited Schumacher to the White House. He installed solar panels on top of the presidential residence (subsequently removed by Reagan). He established a National Center for Appropriate Technology (quickly dismantled by Reagan after he took office). And on 15 July 1979, in Annapolis, he delivered his famous "spiritual malaise" speech, in which he attacked central tenets of the American Dream: self-indulgence and consumption in particular. This was the counter-hegemonic gauntlet.

As one might imagine, it didn't play very well. Carter didn't really know his audience, and he didn't understand that all of those ecological books and phrases didn't really amount to more than cocktail-party chatter: counter-hegemony chic, one might call it. Push come to shove, the American people were never really serious about abandoning the dominant hegemonic paradigm; they just wanted to continue consuming, continue on the path of economic and technological expansion. It is especially noteworthy that in the wake of the speech, several members of Congress took to the floor to suggest that the president had gone mad(!). This is how powerful the American Dream is, the ideology of endless expansion. If you want to break with it, then you *must* be crazy, by definition; what else could explain it? In the Western industrial societies, said Gramsci, counter-hegemony is not likely to defeat hegemony without a long war of attrition. And even then, victory is hardly assured.

So Reagan sailed into office following the greatest presidential landslide in American history. His inauguration ran up a tab of $11 million. His administration tripled the national debt. He never once turned in a balanced budget to Congress. And so on. "Morning in America," he cried; "America is back." No one seemed to mind, and Jimmy returned to his modest house, and his modest lifestyle (which he had never really left). In the presidential election of 2016, the Green Party received 1.06 percent of the popular vote, and zero electoral votes. We now face massive environmental destruction, and are doing nothing about it. To quote W.H. Auden, "We would rather be ruined than changed."

One sociologist—I forget now who it was—described Gramsci as "a theoretician of failure." Politically speaking, he never managed to make anything happen. Did he then wind up in the same place as Machiavelli, with an ideal vision, never to be realized? Perhaps. And yet, both men gave us incredible tools for understanding human beings and human societies; tools for seeing through the dominant mythologies, and how culture relates to power and the status quo. The world is a much richer place for having had Gramsci in it, in my opinion, especially if we reverse Marx's famous dictum: The politicians have changed the world in various ways; the point, however, is to understand it.

Seven

Marinetti: Future Perfect

[The Futurists] have grasped sharply and clearly that our age, the age of big industry, of the large proletarian city and of intense and tumultuous life, was in need of new forms of art, philosophy, behavior and language . . . In their field, the field of culture, the Futurists are revolutionaries.
—Antonio Gramsci, 1921

The Futurist lyricism, a perpetual dynamism of thought, an uninterrupted current of images and sounds, is alone able to express the ephemeral, unstable, and symphonic universe that is forging itself in us and with us.
—F.T. Marinetti, "Let's Murder the Moonshine" (1909)

We have created eternal, omnipresent speed.
—F.T. Marinetti, "The Founding and Manifesto of Futurism" (1909)

Futurism [is] the only artistic movement that can profoundly render the spiritual and aesthetic atmosphere of Fascism.
—F.T. Marinetti, 1932

To explore the life and work of Filippo Tommaso Marinetti is to enter the modern world. It really is a terrible irony: he was a boor and a showman, a warmonger and an imperialist, a fascist down to his death in 1944, and much of his literary output reads like the ravings of a madman—which would not be a totally inaccurate assessment. And yet his historical role in launching *Futurismo*—Futurism—which exalted speed, technology, motion, and "progress"—effectively gave us the world we live in today. Futurism upended the worlds of painting and sculpture, music and literature, theater and cinema, and architecture and urban design, basically transforming the landscape of Western culture. It's not merely, as I said earlier, that genius is neutral; it can also be a package deal, so to speak, in which aspects that are dramatically positive can get enfolded together with ones that are dramatically negative. Such was the case with Marinetti. He launched the movement in 1909; one-hundred-plus years later, *Futurismo* is *Presentismo*, i.e. contemporary modern life.

Marinetti is an example of what Hegel called a "world historical individual" (see Ch. 1)—someone who embodies the spirit of an age and thereby advances it. Such people, Hegel said, were interchangeable: if it hadn't been Napoleon, for example, it would have been someone else. In the early part of the twentieth century, the Futurist outlook was very much in the air, and many individuals who were not, strictly speaking, Futurists— Marcel Duchamp, for example—were nevertheless onto the same idea, often unconsciously. Duchamp's *Nude Descending a Staircase, No. 2* (1912), one of the most famous paintings in the history of art, and which precipitated a major stir when it was exhibited at the 1913 Armory Show in New York, is an attempt to portray motion as it is happening—a mode of perception central to the Futurist world view. Dada and Surrealism followed closely on the heels of Futurism, all being part of (Hegel again) the *zeitgeist,* in which, in one form or another, we are still immersed. Had he lived to see the day, Marinetti would have been perfectly at home with computers and cell phones and bullet trains and skyscrapers and the hectic, high-speed life that characterize our age. In her book on Futurism, Caroline Tisdall relates how, in 1913, Marinetti presented a vision of the environment as "an efficient, fast moving machine, [which had] a technocratic ring to it that strikes a chill in an age that is no longer innocent of the dangers inherent in such a vision." "Noise triumphs and reigns over the sensibilities of man," wrote one leading Futurist, Luigi Russolo, the same year. Maybe that's not such a good thing.(1)

Marinetti was born in Egypt in 1876, and lived there for several years as a child. As a young man, he took a degree at the Sorbonne, and then went on to study law at the Universities of Pavia and Genoa. A few years later his essay, "The Founding and Manifesto of Futurism," hit the front page of *Le Figaro* (20 February 1909), the most prestigious newspaper in all of Europe, launching both the Futurist movement and himself. It became a craze; Marinetti was referred to as "the caffeine of Europe," waking everybody up. Yet truth be told, there was nothing substantively new in the Manifesto; the ideas were derivative, very much a part of the European intellectual scene of the late nineteenth and early twentieth centuries. What, then, was the key to Marinetti's success?(2)

The key had two parts, as it turns out. One was the condition of Italy around this time; the other was Marinetti's unique ability to package the ideas floating around him, the *zeitgeist* referred to above, in a lyrical and bombastic way, one that could not fail to catch the attention of his contemporaries. Indeed, one biographer calls him "one of the great intuitive sleepwalking impresarios of Europe."(3) I'll return to that in a moment. First, let me say a few words about the Italy of Marinetti's time.

The bone in the throat of Italy, perhaps to this day, is the split between North and South. The former was industrializing during the nineteenth century; the latter remained rural and agricultural. With the unification of 1861, the *Resorgimento*, the North (parliament of Piedmont) decided to "unify" the country by force, i.e. to impose its jurisdiction over the South. As a result, the *Resorgimento* was a Potemkin unity; 90 percent of Italy's population was rural, and indifferent to a unification that changed nothing for them except to make things economically worse. Gramsci pointed to the heavy exclusion of the masses from politics, and to the lack of any land reform. Italy remained badly divided between a capitalist North and a semifeudal South. As for the educated classes, they generally looked down on the latter, and failed to do anything to promote genuine unification. In their eyes, Italy appeared to be a lifeless nation, completely bogged down and culturally backward. *Resorgimento* means "renewal" or "rebirth"; this was nowhere to be seen. How was the nation going to turn things around?(4)

Marjorie Perloff, in *The Futurist Moment*, notes that in countries like Italy and Russia, the contrast between old and new was so sharp that it evoked, and encouraged, excess and violence. Russia saw the rise of avant-garde movements such as Constructivism and Rayonism, both influenced by Futurism; and then, of course, there were the revolutions of 1905 and 1917. Marinetti's 1909 Manifesto proclaimed: "We will glorify war—the world's only hygiene." It was the very stagnation of Italy at this time that made such pronouncements attractive, that excited so many people with the notion of "out with the old, in with the new." A good many intellectuals were drawn to Nietzsche rather than Marx; they had little faith that socialism or parliamentary democracy could turn things around. What was needed, they decided, was some form of social and cultural shock therapy, and Marinetti seemed to be the man for the job. When you read his work, writes Andrew Hewitt in *Fascist Modernism*, you get a sense of "the excitement that was fascism." To paraphrase Wilhelm Reich at a later date, fascism was sexy, socialism was not. (5)

A cursory glance at Marinetti's life would lead one to believe that there were two Marinettis: the cultural revolutionary, impresario of innovation in art, music, literature, etc., and the fascist, the ardent supporter of Mussolini's regime. But on closer look, it seems that these are really two halves of an integrated whole. Marinetti himself tirelessly argued that Futurism was the spiritual and esthetic basis of fascism, and this assertion cannot be easily dismissed (although those strictly interested in his artistic side have often tended to do so). As in the case of science, as we discussed in Ch. 5, the methodology is a two-edged sword. The Futurists saw their promotion of speed and technology as a form of liberation, and in the context of a stagnant Italy in the early twentieth century, it probably was—at least for some. But as the century wore on, although there was a strain of the philosophy that was immensely creative, there was another strain that might be called the "soft fascism" of modern life, Max Weber's "iron cage," in which daily life is oppressive, and from which there is no easy escape (save for Dilbert cartoons, I suppose). Futurists and fascists alike loved speed, drama, violence, and technology, and the worship of these things hardly died with Marinetti in 1944, or Mussolini in 1945.

So what were the Futurists actually doing, that managed to get huge numbers of people all worked up? This is where things get difficult. As of 2006, according to one expert on the subject, the number of books and articles on Futurism amounted to more than 3,500 titles.(6) It wouldn't be surprising if that number were way in excess of 4,000, as of this writing. The problem is that Futurism permeated virtually every field of European culture, stretching out to England and eventually, the United States (for example, Joseph Stella and John Cage). To give a faithful account of the Futurist achievement would require hundreds of pages, and perhaps half as many illustrations. And then there is the legacy: the influence on Dada and Surrealism, and on the performance art of the sixties and beyond. What Marinetti unleashed, in short, was a tidal wave of cultural change, and scholars are still struggling to come to terms with what it all means. Since this is a deliberately short book, a book of cameos, as I've said, I must ask the reader's indulgence: I am going to do my best to pick and choose from the vast array of Futurist artifacts.

If Futurism could be summarized in a single word, if it can be said to stand for one single thing, that word would be "rupture." In every area of culture, the works were violent, dynamic, and it is no accident that they led to a host of avant-garde cultural expressions that sought a complete break with the past. Consider the following excerpts from Marinetti's writings:

- "We will destroy the museums, libraries, academies of every kind, we will fight moralism, feminism, every opportunistic or utilitarian cowardice."
- "Let us burn the gondolas, rocking chairs for cretins, and raise to the heavens the imposing geometry of metal bridges and howitzers." (This from his 1910 manifesto, "Against Past-Loving Venice." The manifesto was printed up—800,000 copies' worth—and the leaflets were rained down from the campanile of St. Mark's.)
- "We look for the creation of a nonhuman type in whom moral suffering, goodness of heart, affection, and love...will be abolished." (One hundred years later, it looks like Marinetti got his wish.)
- "One must persecute, lash, torture all those who sin against speed."(7)

Clearly, this was not a well-adjusted individual. At the same time, Marinetti was saying what a lot of his contemporaries believed and wanted, only in neon. And his sense of the future was uncanny: the men of the twenty-first century, he predicted, will "write in books of nickel no thicker than three centimeters, costing no more than eight francs, and still containing one hundred thousand pages." The book as we have known it, he added, is fated to disappear. Marinetti also displayed an interest in the possibility of processed food, and of replacing food with vitamins. As far as the cinema went, he anticipated Fellini: a film will be "a jumble of objects and reality thrown together at random." And in his "Portrait of Mussolini" (1929), he called *Il Duce* (his alter ego, really) a "lyric child armed with lightning intuition." This was no less true of himself.(8)

One individual attracted to the movement was the architect Antonio Sant'Elia, who produced sketches of cities that heavily influenced Le Corbusier, and which became, in effect, our cities. Buildings were designed as vertical towers with external tubular elevator shafts, a formula since imitated in hundreds of hotels around the world. (Plate 19) The Futurists pursued collage, sound poetry, performance art, nonlinear typography, and the music of noise. Giacomo Balla's *Dynamism of a Dog in Motion* (Plate 20), painted the same year as Duchamp's *Nude Descending a Staircase*, had the identical idea: to capture stages of motion in linear sequence, as it was happening. In 1922, Ivo Pannaggi came out with *Speeding Train* (Plate 21), reflecting the Futurist interest in the locomotive as a symbol of motion, and the power of the machine. (Also in 1922, Pannaggi wrote, with Marinetti's assistance, the "Manifesto of Futurist Mechanical Art.") All of this exemplifies the Futurist notion of a world in constant movement.(9)

The Futurists produced more than fifty manifestos during 1909-15, which were read aloud in cities all over Europe, accompanied by noise, drama, gestures, and improvisation. Crowds came prepared: they threw vegetables at the performers. Marinetti often double-booked the seats, to ensure pandemonium, and in some cases sold ten tickets for the same seat. Futurism was a pervasive presence in London from 1910 to 1915, during which time Ezra Pound came under its influence. D.H. Lawrence as well.(10)

Another Futurist, Luigi Russolo, mentioned above, decided that noise had to become part of music, and invented the "Noise Intoners" (*Intonarumori*). These machines were boxes fitted with huge metal speakers. Stravinsky and Diaghilev attended one such "noisy" concert, and apparently loved the effects. One machine, for example, was a "Crackler"; another, a "Rustler." The London Coliseum hosted twelve such events during the summer of 1914, and similar concerts in Paris a few years later made a strong impression on Maurice Ravel. Other musicians who were influenced by Futurist music included John Cage and Sergei Prokofiev.(11)

Much of the Futurist program was characterized by genius, and as must be obvious by now, it drew many geniuses into its orbit. But Marinetti was all over the place; some of what he advocated was just plain nuts. Thus he wrote a Futurist cookbook, in which he rejected pasta(!), and a manifesto on the Italian hat (he was also known to wear an aluminum tie). *La Cucina futurista* (1932) included recipes for smoked camel meat and raw onion ice cream. The recipe for "Steel Chicken" involved stuffing the poor bird with ball bearings, and "The Excited Pig" consisted of a salami propped up in a pool of coffee and cologne. In 2014, at the Guggenheim Museum in New York, a "Tactile Dinner" was served, in which participants wore pajamas decorated with sponges, sandpaper, and aluminum, and ate salads without using any cutlery. As for Marinetti's "Futurist Manifesto of the Italian Hat," he recommended the use of cork, glass, sponge, and neon tubing. While not too many readers of these pages are likely to deck themselves out in sponges and neon tubes, or pop into the Guggenheim in their pajamas for a steaming plate of Steel Chicken, there is something admirable about the sheer dementia of this aspect of Futurism that cannot be denied. (I myself would be willing to wear a Futurist hat, perhaps for a day.)(12)

All of this barely scratches the surface of the Futurist output; it's just too vast, as already indicated. In any case, we've gone from the sublime to the ridiculous; I need to close out this chapter with a further descent, this time into the depraved—Marinetti's embrace of Mussolini. I suggested earlier that a movement such as this is a package deal; it will therefore be important to say a few words about the fascism of Futurism.

Before we deal with the relationship between Marinetti and Mussolini, however, one other relationship, or congruence, needs to be highlighted. This latter is the subject of a brilliant study by the historian Modris Ecksteins, *Rites of Spring*, in which he asserts that there was a "sibling relationship" between the avant-garde in general and fascism. Both movements celebrated vitality, spontaneity, and change—transitoriness, and constant metamorphosis. Nazism, says Ecksteins, was the offspring of a hybrid that formed the modernist impulse: irrationalism and "technicism." Similarly, Andrew Hewitt suggests that we cannot understand the collaboration of avant-garde artists with fascism unless we recognize that both operate under a similar logic, have a similar ideological basis. In particular, fascism easily works within the machine esthetic so energetically promoted by the Futurists. Ultimately, the State is seen as a huge machine.(13)

As for the congruence between Marinetti and Mussolini, it must be said that it was, occasionally, a fractious relationship, and Marinetti even quit the Fascist Party for two years at one point (1920-22). But overall, the relationship was a close one. Marinetti co-authored the Fascist Manifesto, and around 1913 he and Mussolini spoke at the same meetings. In 1918 Marinetti founded the Futurist Political Party; a year later it merged with Mussolini's Fasci Italiani di Combattimento. That same year, Marinetti appeared, alongside Mussolini, on the list of Fascist Party candidates. The Futurist celebration of violence—which was present from Day One—was (for Marinetti and others) embodied and symbolized by Mussolini. Marinetti's innovations in performance influenced the histrionic style of Mussolini's public speeches, and the latter's methods—bombast, threats, disregard for the truth—were techniques he learned from his political colleague. As Caroline Tisdall points out, the two of them were very similar in terms of character and personality. The rhetoric was nearly identical; and both believed in Nietzsche's notion of the Superman, the Man of Destiny. At one point, Mussolini referred to Marinetti as a "fervent Fascist." Futurism, adds Tisdall, was "very much a male club, with a puerile and indeed sinister insistence on aggressive virility." All in all, fascism copied Futurism both in content and in form.(14)

Marinetti did occasionally dissent from Mussolini's policies, but after 1922, when he rejoined the Fascist Party, such objections were merely rhetorical. He became active in Italy's drive for empire, and spoke of Mussolini as though the latter were practically divine. When Mussolini proclaimed a dictatorship in 1925, Marinetti lined up his fellow Futurists to support this move. He was especially keen to propagate the idea that Futurism was the precursor of fascism, that Mussolini was a Futurist, and he published *Futurism and Fascism* in 1924, which he dedicated to *Il Duce*. Step by step, to fall in line with the regime, Marinetti compromised or abandoned most of his previously held positions, including anticlericalism and the importance of individual liberty. He said nothing when Mussolini abolished freedom of the press and assembly, and agreed with him that the purpose of culture was to serve the state. In 1926, Marinetti traveled to South America to promote the fascist cause, and was pronounced an "Honorary Black Shirt" as a result. When, in 1938, Mussolini declared that the Jews were not really Italians, Marinetti made no objection, and in fact sat on a commission to eliminate Jewish writers from Italian bookshelves, targeting 900 of them. He repeatedly asserted that there were no Jews in modern art or in the Futurist movement, and he kept silent when, all around him, the Jews were rounded up and shipped off to Auschwitz—more than a quarter of the entire Jewish population. At one point, Marinetti announced that in his opinion, Hitler was advancing Futurist principles.(15)

Mussolini was deposed and arrested in July of 1943; in September, Hitler had him sprung from prison and set him up as the puppet leader of the German-run Salò Republic in Northern Italy. As for Marinetti, he lived out his remaining months in the service of Salò, and when Rome was liberated by the Allies in June of 1944, he fled to Bellagio, where he died six months later. He wrote a final poem praising the vicious Black Brigades, which, by the end of the war, were deemed war criminals for the atrocities they had committed. Upon his death, Mussolini held a state funeral for this hero of fascism in Milan. Mussolini himself died the following year, shot by Italian partisans and strung up, upside down, at the Piazzale Loreto in Milan, for the Italian people to spit on, shoot, and beat with hammers.(16)

So there you have it: the man who spawned some of the most creative movements of the twentieth century, who can almost be said to have *launched* the twentieth century, turns out to have been a coward, a toady, and—truth be told—a despicable human being. History has a funny way of being unpredictable and nonlinear, *n'est-ce pas?* How to explain such a thing, if it can be explained at all?

The fact is, it was not entirely opportunism or a lust for power on Marinetti's part, that was driving him. What Modris Ecksteins argues is profoundly correct: there really *is* a congruence between fascism and the avant-garde. What do you think is going to happen if you endlessly glorify war, violence, the machine, the irrational, and the anti-human? If the past, in your mind, counts for nothing, and "rupture" for everything? The connection between Futurism and fascism that Marinetti kept proselytizing for was no fantasy, no illusion. Rather, it was right there, in the rhetoric, the documents, the physical style, and the ideology. *Genio* is great—fabulous, in fact—but ultimately, context is just as important.

And so I end this book on a sober note. We have seen the supreme artistry of Bernini and Caravaggio and Fellini, been awed by the humanity of St. Francis, amazed by the subtlety of Machiavelli, and admiring of the courage and insightfulness of Gramsci. And then we have Marinetti, the joker in the pack, whose advancement of culture was astonishing, and—integrally related to this—whose "contributions to the darker side of the last century," observes one of his biographers, "are . . . unquestionable." (17) *Fine, amici*; end of story.

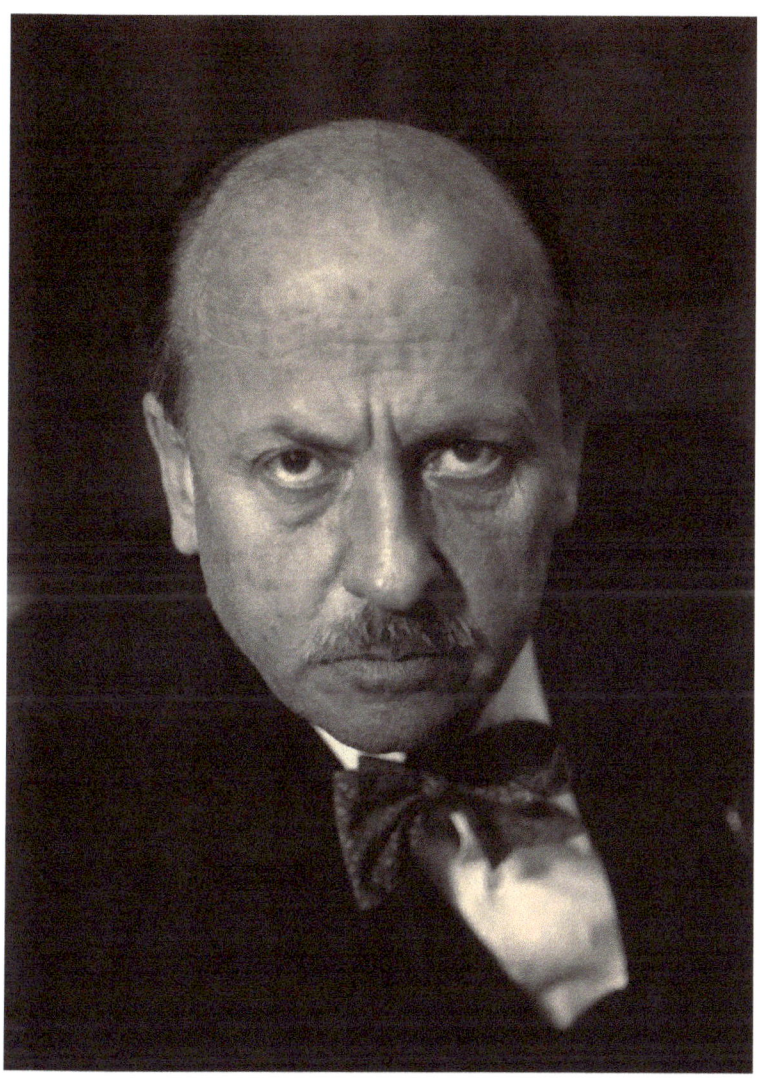

18. Filippo Tommaso Marinetti

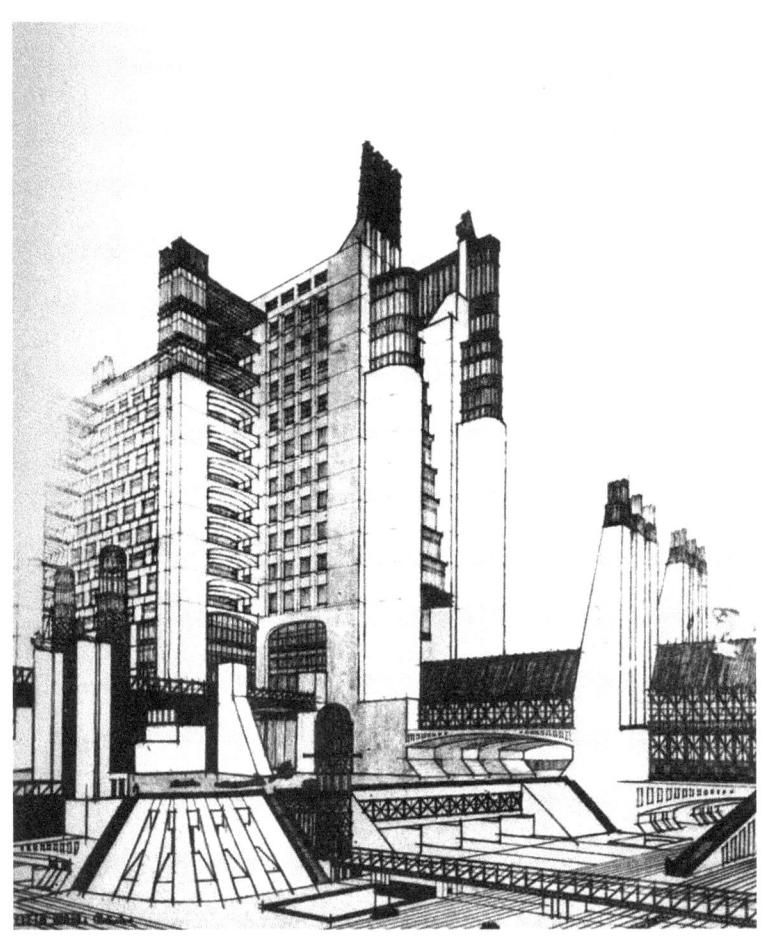

19. Antonio Sant'Elia, *La Città nuova*

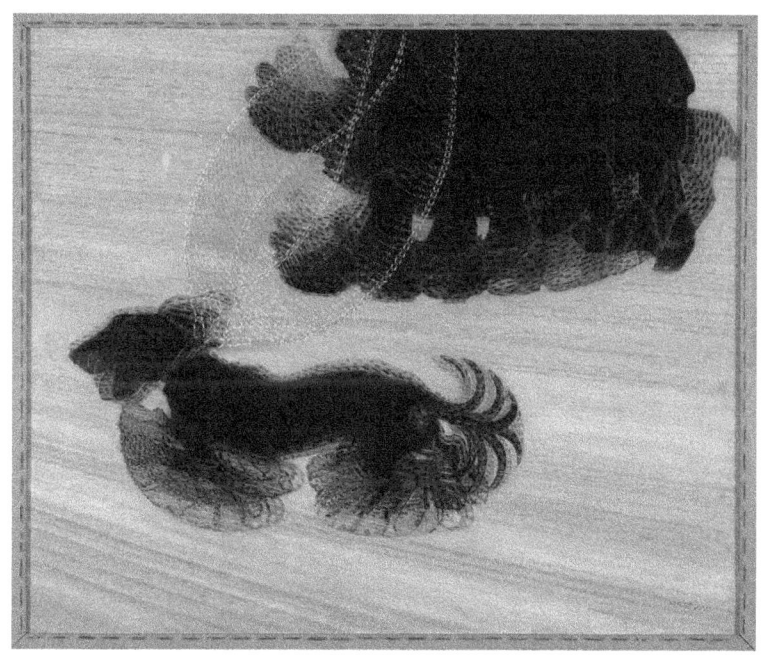

20. Giacomo Balla, *Dynamism of a Dog in Motion*

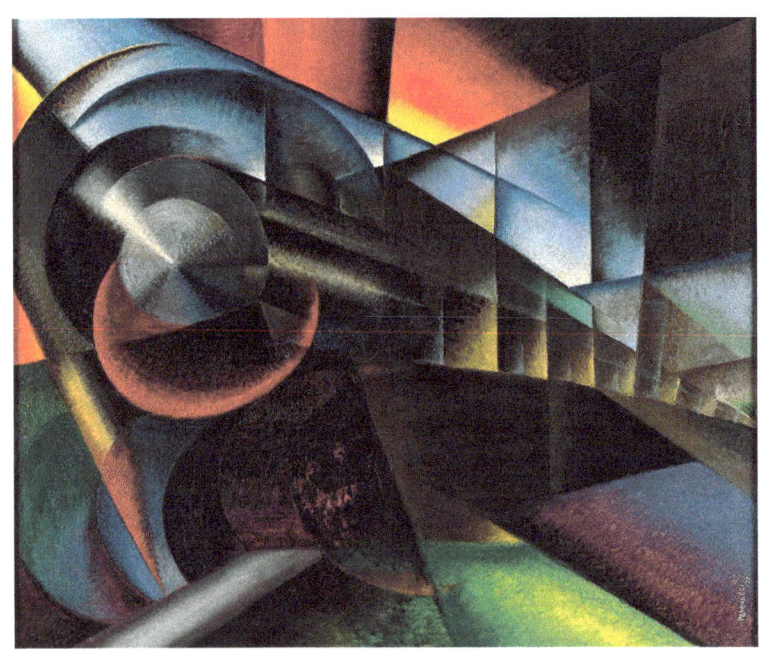

21. Ivo Pannaggi, *Speeding Train*

Epilogue: My Italy

As the reader may have guessed by now, this subject, that of the genius of Italian culture, is a very personal one for me. Much of my life, probably since my teenage years, has been dominated by two archetypes: indulgence and austerity. The latter, for me, is embodied in the craft and meditative traditions of Japan. I love that aspect of Japanese culture, and wrote about it in a book I published several years ago called *Neurotic Beauty*. The whole notion of restraint and self-discipline, *satori* and self-knowledge, is one we in the West could surely use a large dose of; and for a number of years I studied Aikido, played Go, sat *zazen*, read haiku, and so on. For the most part, I failed in my attempt to achieve a centered austerity, and I suspect it's something I shall always have to struggle with.

As for indulgence, that to my mind was clearly about Italy: expansive, hedonistic, in love with the world: *la dolce vita*, the Sistine Chapel, the Palazzo Vecchio, huge platters of spaghetti bolognese, the sun-drenched streets of Sicily. Of course, it might be argued that St. Francis and Antonio Gramsci don't quite fit the model, and yet in a way, I think they do. Both of them, just like Bernini and the rest, bit off life in large chunks, went at it head on, and left the world a better place (Marinetti possibly excepted). There is something glorious about all of this dynamism, *non è vero?* It brings to mind Alexandre Koyré's characterization of the Galilean achievement: *From the Closed World to the Infinite Universe*. This is what I mean when I talk about transformation and "creating space." Leonardo and his flying machines, Giordano Bruno and his infinite worlds...the *excessiveness* of it all. "Nothing succeeds like excess," quipped Oscar Wilde, and Italian culture is nothing if not successful, even allowing for the dark side of its history.

There is, however, no great moral to this story, no transcendent message. In an interview he once did for the *Corriere della Sera*, Fellini told the reporter: "I'll tell you the truth: everything I did in my life I did out of pure enjoyment." (No dummy, he.) All I wanted to do in writing this book, gentle reader, was to serve up the intellectual equivalent of spaghetti bolognese, and the sun-drenched streets of Sicily, for you to enjoy. I hope I succeeded.

NOTES

Preface

1. My epiphany was somewhat deflated a few months later when I discovered that Bernini had farmed out the carving of the fine detail of the statue to Giuliano Finelli, a man working in his studio. The tale of Apollo and Daphne goes back a long way in Greek mythology, ultimately to be "updated" by Ovid in his book *Metamorphoses*. Bernini worked off of Ovid's version, so even the concept of the statue cannot said to have been his. And yet, the psychology of the work, its spiritual energy, so to speak, is definitely Bernini's. Spirituality in art is a Bernini trademark, his overriding passion; and in the case of much of his work, this got expressed in terms of movement and transformation. But if he was not personally involved in the fine material details, we have to credit Finelli for his ability to make his master's vision manifest. The "translation" of hair into bay leaves, carried out in hard and brittle marble—brilliant craftsmanship, in a word—is as epiphanic, I believe, as the psychology of the work. In the last analysis, the sculpture has to be seen as a complementary, or collaborative, effort, because it's the two things working together that make *Apollo and Daphne* what it is. See Charles Scribner III, *Bernini* (NY: Harry N. Abrams, 1991), pp. 18 and 64; Jennifer Montagu, *Roman Baroque Sculpture* (New Haven: Yale University Press, 1989), pp. 99, 102, 104, and 106-7; and Franco Mormando, *Bernini: His Life and His Rome* (Chicago: University of Chicago Press, 2011), pp. 44-45.
2. Isaiah Berlin, *Vico and Herder* (New York: Viking, 1976), p. 55.

Chapter 1

1. Franco Mormando, *Bernini: His Life and His Rome* (Chicago: University of Chicago Press, 2011), p. 62; Wikipedia, articles "Baroque" and "Bernini"; Rudolf Wittkower, *Art and Architecture in Italy 1600-1750* (5th ed.; New Haven: Yale University Press, 1982; orig. publ. 1958), p. 140.

2. Charles Scribner III, *Bernini* (New York: Harry N. Abrams, 1991), pp. 15 and 50; Mormando, *Bernini*, p. 96; and Wittkower, *Art and Architecture*, pp. 144, 154, and 169.

3. Scribner, *Bernini*, pp. 15, 64, 66, and 78; Wikipedia, article "Baroque."

4. Mormando, *Bernini*, pp. 40, 43; Wikipedia, article "Bernini."

5. Mary E. Barnard, *The Myth of Apollo and Daphne from Ovid to Quevedo* (Durham NC: Duke University Press, 1987); Hamish Bowles, *Vogue,* 15 November 2017: https://www.vogue.com/article/hamish-bowles-bernini-borghese-rome

6. Bowles, *Vogue*, 15 November 2017; Wittkower, *Art and Architecture*, p. 145; Howard Hibbard, "Gian Lorenzo Bernini," *Encyclopaedia Britannica*: https://www.britannica.com/biography/Gian-Lorenzo-Bernini#ref120313

7. Wittkower, *Art and Architecture*, pp. 140 and 169; Simon Schama, BBC documentary, "Power of Art," section on Bernini; Mormando, *Bernini*, pp. 161 and 164.

8. Scribner, Bernini, pp. 80 and 108; Wittkower, Art and Architecture, p. 169; Mormando, Bernini, pp. 64 and 71; Artble: https://artble.com/artists/gian_lorenzo_bernini

Chapter 2

1. Andrew Graham-Dixon, *Caravaggio: A Life Sacred and Profane* (New York: W.W. Norton, 2010), p. 3.

2. Wikipedia, article "Caravaggio."

3. Charles Scribner III, *Bernini* (New York: Harry N. Abrams, 1991), dust jacket and pp. 8 and 48.

4. Graham-Dixon, *Caravaggio*, pp. 93-96.

5. Ibid., pp. 98-100 and 104-5; Helen Langdon, *Caravaggio: A Life* (New York: Farrar, Straus and Giroux, 1998), pp. 85 and 92-93.
6. Graham-Dixon, *Caravaggio*, pp. 117 and 194-96.
7. Ibid., pp. 196-97; Langdon, *Caravaggio*, p. 176.
8. Graham-Dixon, *Caravaggio*, pp. 325 and 332-35.
9. Ibid., pp. 332-33 and Simon Schama, BBC documentary, "Power of Art," section on Caravaggio.
10. Graham-Dixon, *Caravaggio*, pp. 151, 202, 232, 439, and 441; Wikipedia, article "Caravaggio"; and Rudolf Wittkower, *Art and Architecture in Italy 1600-1750* (5th ed.; New Haven: Yale University Press, 1982; orig. publ. 1958), p. 56.

Chapter 3

1. The following sketch is taken from Wikipedia, article "Fellini," which in turn is based on a number of sources, several of which I also used, such as Kezich and Bondanella (see below).
2. Quoted in Peter Bondanella, *The Cinema of Federico Fellini* (Princeton: Princeton University Press, 1992), p. 152.
3. Federico Fellini, *Fellini on Fellini*, trans. Isabel Quigley (Boston: Da Capo Press, 1996; orig. publ. 1976), p. 51; Bondanella, *Cinema of Federico Fellini*, p. 20. At one point Fellini referred to "film, whose allure is motion, rhythm, dynamic[*sic*]"; see Milo Manara and Federico Fellini, *Trip to Tulum,* trans. E. Bell and S. Gaudiano (New York: Catalan Communications, 1990), p. 6.
4. *Fellini on Fellini*, pp. 58, 103, and 147; Tullio Kezich, *Federico Fellini*, trans. Minna Proctor and Viviana Mazza (New York: Faber and Faber, 2006), p. 3.
5. Kezich, *Federico Fellini*, p. 41; Bondanella, *Cinema of Federico Fellini*, p. xxi.
6. Bondanella, *Cinema of Federico Fellini*, p. 113.
7. On this and the following paragraph see ibid., pp. 105 and 107, and Kezich, *Federico Fellini*, p. 157. Verge of tears: Fellini

initially brought the script to producer Luigi Rovere, who read it and began to weep. See Wikipedia, article "La Strada."

8. Commentaries of Scorsese and Bondanella, attached to the DVD of the film; Calvino quoted in Bondanella, *Cinema of Federico Fellini*, pp. 9-10.

9. Bondanella, *Cinema of Federico Fellini*, pp. 103-4 and 332; Wikipedia, article "La Strada."

10. Bondanella, *Cinema of Federico Fellini*, p. 115.

11. Ibid., pp. 101 and 103; Scorsese and Bondanella, commentaries; Kezich, *Federico Fellini*, pp. 156-57; and Wikipedia, article "La Strada."

12. Wikipedia, article "La Strada."

13. This and the next two paragraphs are taken from Wikipedia, article "La Dolce Vita," and Bondanella, *Cinema of Federico Fellini*, pp. 133-36, 141, and 145.

14. Kezich, *Federico Fellini*, pp. 202-3; Bondanella, *Cinema of Federico Fellini*, pp. 141-42.

15. Bondanella, *Cinema of Federico Fellini*, pp. 132 and 146-49.

16. Kezich, *Federico Fellini*, pp. 205, 208, and 212-13.

17. Ibid., pp. 224 and 227.

18. This and the next two paragraphs are taken from Wikipedia, article "8½"; see also Bondanella, *Cinema of Federico Fellini*, pp. 163-77, and Kezich, *Federico Fellini*, pp. 234 and 239.

19. Bondanella, *Cinema of Federico Fellini*, p. 171.

20. Kezich, *Federico Fellini*, pp. 242 and 245-50.

Chapter 4

1. This story has been told many times over, in dozens of biographies. My own sources for this chapter are Wikipedia, article "Francis of Assisi"; André Vauchez, *Francis of Assisi*, trans. Michael Cusato (New Haven: Yale University Press, 2012); Donald Spoto, *Reluctant Saint* (New York: Penguin, 2002); Murray Bodo, *Francis: The Journey and the Dream* (Cincinnati:

Franciscan Media, 2011; Orig. publ. 1971); G.K. Chesterton, *Saint Francis of Assisi* (New York: Image Books, 1957; orig. publ. 1924); and Joan Acocella, "Rich Man, Poor Man," *New Yorker*, 14 January 2013.

2. Morris Berman, *Wandering God* (Albany: SUNY Press, 2000); Bodo, *Francis*, pp. 48 and 133.

3. Vauchez, *Francis of Assisi*, pp. 73 and 79-80.

4. Spoto, *Reluctant Saint*, p. 197. For a very fine novel that treats the topic of stigmata with great sensitivity, see Ron Hansen, *Mariette in Ecstasy* (New York: Harper Perennial, 1992).

5. Vauchez, *Francis of Assisi*, pp. 245 and 320; Helen Langdon, *Caravaggio: A Life* (New York: Farrar, Straus and Giroux, 1998), pp. 3 and 16. The historian referred to is Paul Sabatier, who published his *Life of Saint Francis* during 1893-94.

6. Vauchez, *Francis of Assisi*, pp. 275 and 281.

7. G.K. Chesterton, *Saint Francis of Assisi*, p. 89.

8. Peter Bondanella, *The Cinema of Federico Fellini* (Princeton: Princeton University Press, 1992), p. 52.

Chapter 5

1. Leo Strauss, *Thoughts on Machiavelli* (Glencoe IL: The Free Press, 1958); Quentin Skinner, *Machiavelli: A Very Short Introduction* (Oxford: Oxford University Press, 2000; orig. publ. 1981). A third school of thought is that Machiavelli was really a republican (see below, esp. n.9), although this can be seen to overlap with the "scientific" school to some extent. There is also a subset of the "republican" school that believes that *The Prince* is a work of deliberate irony—tongue-in-cheek, as it were. This is most closely identified, in recent times, with Erica Benner, *Machiavelli's Prince: A New Reading* (Oxford: Oxford University Press, 2014), and *Be Like the Fox* (New York: W.W. Norton, 2017). Antecedents include Spinoza and Rousseau.

2. Wikipedia, article "Niccolò Machiavelli"; Miles Unger, *Machiavelli* (New York: Simon & Schuster, 2011), p. 54. Cf. Paul Oppenheimer, *Machiavelli* (London: Continuum, 2011), p. 244: "The conspicuous themes of [*The Prince*] are its uncompromising naturalism and its empirical approach to reality."

3. For a fuller elaboration of this argument see my *Reenchantment of the World* (Ithaca NY: Cornell University Press, 1981). As for the comparison with Galileo, Unger writes: "Galileo, like Machiavelli, was able to topple millennia-old systems of belief through the power of direct observation" (*Machiavelli*, p. 257n). See also Leonardo Olschki, *Machiavelli the Scientist* (Berkeley: The Gillick Press, 1945), pp. 22-33.

4. Arthur Koestler, *The Sleepwalkers* (London: Hutchinson, 1959).

5. Wikipedia, article "Niccolò Machiavelli." The nineteenth-century historian Francesco de Sanctis wrote that Machiavelli represents "the most profound negation of the Middle Ages" (quoted in Benedetto Fontana, *Hegemony and Power* [Minneapolis: University of Minnesota Press, 1993], p. 53).

6. Niccolò Machiavelli, *The Prince*, trans. Luigi Ricci, rev. ed. E.R.P. Vincent (New York: New American Library, 1952), p. 84.

7. On this and the following paragraph see Skinner, *Machiavelli*, pp. 40-46, 51, and 53, and Machiavelli, *Prince*, p. 90. For an interesting discussion of a similar inversion of "virtue" in America in the late eighteenth century, see Joyce Appleby, *Capitalism and a New Social Order* (New York: NYU Press, 1984).

8. Machiavelli, *Prince*, p. 94.

9. Strauss,*Thoughts*, p. 292; Wikipedia, article "Niccolò Machiavelli"; Giovanni Giorgini, "Five Hundred Years of Italian Scholarship on Machiavelli's 'Prince'," *The Review of Politics*, vol.

75 no. 4 (Fall 2013), pp. 632-33; and Benner, *Be Like the Fox*. I should add that a number of scholars see a unity of thought between *The Prince* and the *Discourses,* rather than a divergence of emphasis, but this is a long-standing debate. The classic argument (in English) for divergence, and the superiority/republicanism of the *Discourses* is Hans Baron, "Machiavelli: the Republican Citizen and the Author of 'The Prince'," *English Historical Review*, vol. 76 no. 299 (April 1961), pp. 217-53. John Najemy, in a penetrating review of Baron's analysis, points out that Baron evaded the issue that Machiavelli did not: that there were "political and ideological links that bound the civic humanists to the ruling oligarchy"; that as important as republicanism was, the ideas of the humanists needed to be seen as ideology, and therefore "as a strategically pursued legitimation of the ruling group." Baron believed that the "real" Machiavelli was a republican, but Machiavelli was aware of—and one might add, ambiguous about—the fact that republican politics were hardly pure, and that "social conflict, ideological manipulation, and hegemonic ambition" were central to them. At the same time, the notion of political liberty lies at the heart of the *Discourses*, and Baron was right to assert that the dominant theme of this work is the view of "the moral health and political vigour of a free nation as the ultimate source of power" (Baron, "Machiavelli," p. 224). In any event, scholars keep asking, "Will the real Machiavelli please stand up?", but the answer might possibly be "all of them." See John Najemy, "Baron's Machiavelli and Renaissance Republicanism," *The American Historical Review*, vol. 101 no. 1 (February 1996), pp. 119-29. On contradictory interpretations of Machiavelli see Eric Cochrane, "Machiavelli: 1940-1960," *Journal of Modern History*, vol. 33 no. 2 (June 1961), pp. 114-36, and Isaiah Berlin, "The Question of Machiavelli," *New York Review of Books*, 4 November 1971. Berlin quotes

Benedetto Croce (see below) as saying that the case of Machiavelli "will perhaps never be closed."

10. Benner, *Be Like the Fox*, pp. 270-77, 284, and 290.

11. Skinner, *Machiavelli*, pp. 59, 61, and 85; Baron, "Machiavelli," p. 250. On Machiavelli's ambiguity see n.9, above.

12. Benner, *Be Like the Fox*, p. xvi; Giorgini, "Five Hundred Years," p. 636; Benedetto Croce, *Etica e politica* (Bari: Laterza, 1981; orig. publ. 1931); Berlin, "Question of Machiavelli." Machiavelli on St. Francis: see above, Ch. 4, and Unger, *Machiavelli*, p. 301. Fontana, however (see above, n. 5), argues that Croce saw Machiavelli as amoral/scientific (*Hegemony and Power*, p. 185, n.7; references on debates over the moral question are cited in n.8).

13. Unger, *Machiavelli*, pp. 132, 215, 238, and 331. Equally revealing, perhaps, is his statement that the *Discourses* were dedicated "not to those who are princes, but [to] those who, on account of their innumerable good qualities, deserve to be" (quoted on p. 284, and see also Fontana, *Hegemony and Power*, p. 192). Unger also claims (pp. 349-50) that Machiavelli had no politics as such, i.e. did not subscribe to any particular political creed.

14. Wikipedia, article "Niccolò Machiavelli." On an unrelated matter, I have omitted any reference to the issue of physical movement in Machiavelli's life, which was no less significant for him as it was for Bernini, Caravaggio, Fellini, and St. Francis, so let me provide a brief summary here. Machiavelli was tireless, energetic from childhood. He even wrote a long poem called *The Ass*, in which he has a character (a boy) who is constantly "running through the street, and at any time, without any heed." As long as he lived, wrote Machiavelli, he ran. In his writings, Machiavelli frequently stressed the importance of an active life, pointing out that motion meant activity and change. He held a number of important government posts, including

Florentine Secretary, and wound up on horseback much of the time on foreign and military missions for the city of Florence as well as for the pope. Thus in 1502, he rode out to the city of Imola (in the Romagna) to negotiate with Cesare Borgia, having to stay there much longer than expected. His coworker back in Florence, Agostino Vespucci (brother of the more famous Amerigo), finally fed up with his absence, wrote him somewhat angrily, referring to "that spirit of yours, so eager for riding, wandering, and roaming about." This was a fair characterization. Machiavelli, says de Grazia, was "as active a man as one can find." All of this was congruent with his assertion in the *Discourses*, that "all affairs of this world are in motion and will not remain fixed." See de Grazia, *Machiavelli in Hell*, pp. 20, 195, 242, 250, 286, and 343; Benner, *Be Like the Fox,* pp. 161 and 294-95; and Oppenheimer, *Machiavelli*, p. 250.

Chapter 6

1. Giuseppe Fiori, *Antonio Gramsci: Life of a Revolutionary*, trans. Tom Nairn (New York: E.P. Dutton, 1971), pp. 16 and 237. For the *Quaderni del carcere*, or Prison Notebooks, see Quintin Hoare and Geoffrey Nowell Smith (eds. and trans.), *Selections from the Prison Notebooks* (New York: International Publishers, 1989 reprint ed.). As in the case of Machiavelli, there are many different versions or interpretations of what Gramsci was saying. For an overview of the various "Gramscis," see Chantal Mouffe (ed.), *Gramsci and Marxist Theory* (London: Routledge & Kegan Paul, 1979).

2. Karl Marx and Friedrich Engels, *Manifesto of the Communist Party*, in Lewis Feuer (ed.), *Marx & Engels: Basic Writings on Politics and Philosophy* (Garden City NY: Anchor Books, 1959), p. 9.

3. Marx and Engels, "Excerpts from *The German Ideology*," in Feuer, *Marx & Engels*, p. 247.

4. Marx and Engels, *Manifesto*, in Feuer, *Marx & Engels*, p. 26; Isaiah Berlin, *Karl Marx* (3rd ed.: New York: Oxford University Press, 1963; orig. publ. 1939), pp. 139-40; Erich Fromm, *Escape from Freedom* (New York: Holt Paperbacks, 1994; orig. publ. 1941); and Nicole Aschoff, *The New Prophets of Capital* (London: Verso, 2015), p. 2.

5. Marx was a lot more flexible, and a lot less deterministic, than I have portrayed him here. He did recognize the complexity of the superstructure, and saw that it had some degree of independence from the base. On this point (among others), there proved to be a big difference between him and his followers, such that he once remarked, "Je ne suis pas une marxiste." Inasmuch as this issue has been the subject of several hundred books, I've decided to sidestep it in this discussion. The philosopher and historian Norberto Bobbio argued, in 1967, that Gramsci had actually inverted Marx, making the superstructure more significant than the base. See Mouffe, *Gramsci and Marxist Theory*, pp. 3 and 21-47.

6. Gwyn Williams, "The Concept of 'Egemonia' in the Thought of Antonio Gramsci: Some Notes on Interpretation," *Journal of the History of Ideas*, vol. 21 no. 4 (Oct.-Dec. 1960), p. 587.

7. Niccolò Machiavelli, *The Prince*, trans. Luigi Ricci, rev. ed. E.R.P. Vincent (New York: New American Library, 1952), p. 92; Perry Anderson, "The Antinomies of Antonio Gramsci," *New Left Review*, I/100 (Nov.-Dec. 1976), pp. 20, 49, and 49n; and Gramsci, *Prison Notebooks*, pp. 169-70.

8. Williams, "Concept of 'Egemonia'," p. 591.

9. George Hoare and Nathan Sperber, *An Introduction to Antonio Gramsci* (London: Bloomsbury, 2016), pp. 2, 29, 47, 56, 122, and 124; Fiori, *Antonio Gramsci*, pp. 238 and 243; Benedetto Fontana, *Hegemony and Power* (Minneapolis: University of Minnesota Press, 1993), pp. 141 and 143; Wikipedia, article "Antonio Gramsci"; Thomas Bates, "Gramsci and the Theory of

Hegemony," *Journal of the History of Ideas,*" vol. 36 no. 2 (Apr.-Jun. 1975), pp. 352-56, 360, and 365; and Anderson, "Antinomies," pp. 22 and 26-27.

10. Walter Adamson, "Gramsci's Interpretation of Fascism," *Journal of the History of Ideas*, vol. 41 no. 4 (Oct.-Dec. 1980), pp. 631-32; Gramsci, *Prison Notebooks*, pp. 139-40.

11. On this and the following paragraphs see Hoare and Sperber, *Introduction to Gramsci*, pp. 33-41; Williams, "Concept of 'Egemonia'," pp. 592-94; Fiori, *Antonio Gramsci*, pp. 103-4 and 210-11; Marcia Landy, "Culture and Politics in the Work of Antonio Gramsci ," *boundary 2*, vol. 14 no. 3 (Spring 1986), p. 53; and Gramsci, *Prison Notebooks*, pp. 5-10 and 16.

12. Hoare and Sperber, *Introduction to Gramsci*, pp. 130-31; Gramsci, *Prison Notebooks*, pp. 333ff.

13. Bates, "Gramsci and the Theory of Hegemony," pp. 359-60.

14. On American mythologies see the first essay in my *Question of Values* (Charleston SC: CreateSpace, 2010). Discussion that follows is taken from my *Why America Failed* (John Wiley & Sons, 2011), and Christopher Ketcham, "The Fallacy of Endless Economic Growth," *Pacific Standard* (psmag.com), 16 May 2017.

15. I was unfortunately unable to locate the Pew Charitable Trust poll, but here are the results of a Gallup poll, saying much the same thing: https://news.gallup.com/poll/154619/Americans-Having-Rich-Class-Years-Ago.aspx According to a GlobeScan poll of 2012, 58% of Americans said that they felt that the rich among them deserved their wealth: https://globescan.com/public-remains-concerned-over-wealth-inequalities-global-poll/. This probably reflects the various studies that reveal that a large percentage of Americans believe they will eventually realize the American Dream and enter the ranks of the rich, even though the objective conditions would indicate that this is unlikely. There are numerous articles on the patriotism of the poor; e.g., Francesco Duina, "The Patriotism of the Poor," October 2017,

posted at http://stanfordpress.typepad.com/blog/2017/10/the-patriotism-of-the-poor.html.
16. Donella Meadows et al., *Limits to Growth* (New York: Signet, 1972).
17. Donella Meadows et al., *Limits to Growth: The 30-Year Update* (3d ed.; Chelsea VT: Chelsea Green Publishing, 2004).

Chapter 7
1. Caroline Tisdall and Angelo Bozzolla, *Futurism* (London: Thames and Hudson, 1977), pp. 111 and 124.
2. Wikipedia, article "Filippo Tommaso Marinetti"; R.W. Flint, Introduction to R.W. Flint (ed.), *Marinetti: Selected Writings*, trans. R.W. Flint and Arthur A. Coppotelli (New York: Farrar, Straus and Giroux, 1972), p. 6; and Christine Poggi, *Inventing Futurism* (Princeton: Princeton University Press, 2009), p. 12. In *The Futurist Moment* (Chicago: University of Chicago Press, 1986), pp. 84-85, Marjorie Perloff notes how common Marinetti's views were by 1909, the year of his founding Manifesto. His ideas come straight out of Nietzsche, Bergson, Sorel, and Alfred Jarry. There were also several manifestos written by Saint-Georges de Bouhélier (1897), Jules Romain (1905), and Ernst Ludwig Kirschner (1906), which anticipated themes that turned up in Marinetti's texts. Poggi also notes (pp. 10-11) the heavy influence of Mario Morasso's 1905 book, *La nuova arma (La macchina) (The New Weapon: [The Car])*, which exalted the fusion of flesh and metal as a source of regeneration, an idea that became central to Futurism. (See Ch. 5 of her book for further elaboration.) Also noteworthy is the fact that the notion of war as "the world's only hygiene" (a line from the 1909 Manifesto; see below) was very much in the air as events moved inexorably toward World War I. In *In Bluebeard's Castle* (London: Faber & Faber, 1971), George Steiner argues that the Great War was brought on by the "boredom" of the long peace, 1789-1914

(leaving the Napoleonic Wars aside), such that Europeans were itching for something to break the "tedium." Bertrand Russell observed the "itch" finally getting scratched down at Trafalgar Square in 1914, when war was finally declared, and sheer ecstasy ensued. (See my *Wandering God* [Albany: SUNY Press, 2000], p. 12.) Steiner and Russell may not have known it, but the "boredom" argument regarding war was originally made by Machiavelli in 1513. (See Paul Oppenheimer, *Machiavelli* [London: Continuum, 2012], pp. 236-37.)

3. Flint, Introduction, p. 6.

4. Emil Oestereicher, "Fascism and the Intellectuals: The Case of Italian Futurism," *Social Research*, vol. 41 no. 3 (Fall 1974), pp. 515-17 and 522; Wikipedia, article "Italian unification."

5. Wikipedia, article "Rayonism"; Oestereicher, "Fascism and the Intellectuals," pp. 520, 523-25, and 529-33; Andrew Hewitt, *Fascist Modernism* (Stanford: Stanford University Press, 1993), p. 4; and Perloff, *Futurist Moment*, p. xxiii. See also n.2, above. Poggi, in *Inventing Futurism*, argues that the shock of modernity, and the instability of the times, threw identities into major confusion, such that great numbers of people were desperately searching for a dogma, an all-encompassing Answer or new belief system, and that Futurism offered to fill that existential gap. This would seem to mesh well with the historical analysis provided above, and the zeal generated by and for Futurism suggests that she is probably right.

6. Günter Berghaus, "Review: New Research on Futurism and its Relations with the Fascist Regime," *Journal of Contemporary History*, vol. 42 no. 1 (Jan. 2007), p. 149.

7. Quoted in Flint, *Marinetti*, pp. 42, 55, 91, and 95.

8. Ibid., pp. 105, 130-31, and 158-59; Wikipedia, article "Filippo Tommaso Marinetti."

9. Perloff, *Futurist Moment*, pp. xix-xxi and 8; Tisdall, *Futurism*, pp. 107-8 and 124-35.

10. Perloff, *Futurist Moment*, pp. 90, 106-7, 112, 172-73, and 178; Tisdall, *Futurism*, pp. 13, 92, and 102; Wikipedia, article "Filippo Tommaso Marinetti."

11. Tisdall, *Futurism*, pp. 111 and 117-19: Wikipedia, article "Filippo Tommaso Marinetti." On the influence of Futurism on music, including innovations such as atonality, see Mark A. Radice, "'Futurismo:' Its Origins, Context, Repertory, and Influence," *The Musical Quarterly,* vol. 73 no. 1 (1989), pp. 1-17.

12. Wikipedia, article "Filippo Tommaso Marinetti"; Jerry Adler, "Back to the Future," *New Yorker*, 6 September 2004, pp. 101-5.

13. Modris Ecksteins, *Rites of Spring* (Boston: Houghton Mifflin, 1989), pp. xvi, 31, and 303; Hewitt, *Fascist Modernism*, pp. 52, 144, and 164.

14. Wikipedia, article "Filippo Tommaso Marinetti"; Anne Bowler, "Politics as Art: Italian Futurism and Fascism," *Theory and Society*, vol. 20 no. 6 (Dec. 1991), pp. 763, 776, 784-85, and 794n.76; Ernest Ialongo, *Filippo Tommaso Marinetti* (Madison WI: Farleigh Dickinson University Press, 2015), p. 1; and Tisdall, *Futurism*, p. 157. Tisdall's observation receives extended treatment in Poggi, *Inventing Futurism* (see n.2, above), based on Freudian-feminist theory, which she admits (p. 31) is "a series of speculations." Nevertheless, these are often very persuasive speculations.

15. Ialongo, *Filippo Tommaso Marinetti*, pp. 12, 22, 29, 126, 137, 153, 157, 173, 201-3, 269, 281, and 295-96.

16. Ibid., pp. 92-93 and 297-98; Tisdall, *Futurism*, pp. 208-9; Wikipedia, article "Death of Benito Mussolini."

17. Ialongo, *Filippo Tommaso Marinetti*, p. 309.

ABOUT THE AUTHOR

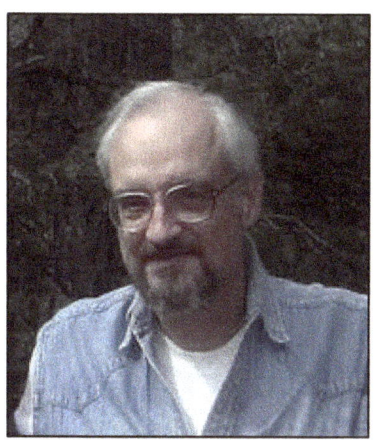

Morris Berman is a poet, novelist, essayist, social critic, and cultural historian. He has written fifteen books and nearly 200 articles, and has taught at a number of universities in Europe, North America, and Mexico. He won the Governor's Writers Award for Washington State in 1990, and was the first recipient of the annual Rollo May Center Grant for Humanistic Studies in 1992. In 2000, *The Twilight of American Culture* was named a "Notable Book" by the *New York Times,* and in 2013 he received the Neil Postman Award for Career Achievement in Public Intellectual Activity from the Media Ecology Association. Dr. Berman lives in Mexico.

www.ingramcontent.com/pod-product-compliance
Lightning Source LLC
Chambersburg PA
CBHW040517220526
45473CB00012B/2891